GW00578192

Other Books by Eve Babitz

TWO *by* TWO

Tango, Two-Step, and the L.A. Night

EVE BABITZ

Simon & Schuster

SIMON & SCHUSTER
Rockefeller Center
1230 Avenue of the Americas
New York, New York 10020

Simon & Schuster and colophon are registered trademarks
of Simon & Schuster, Inc.

Designed by Jeanette Olender
Manufactured in the United States of America

1   3   5   7   9   10   8   6   4   2

Library of Congress Cataloging-in-Publication Data
Babitz, Eve.
Two by two : tango, two-step, and the L.A. night / Eve Babitz.
p.   cm.
Includes index.
1. Ballroom dancing—California—Los Angeles—Anecdotes. 2. Ballroom
dancing—Social aspects—California—Los Angeles. I. Title.
GV1746.B24   1999
306.4'84—dc21   99-38228   CIP
ISBN 978-1-5011-1145-7

ACKNOWLEDGMENTS

Thank you to Maurice Schwartzman,
Renée Victor, Paul McClure, the
Stevens sisters, and all the others
suffering for the art of dance.

Thanks also to the Buena Vista
Social Club (and Ry Cooder)
for reminding us what slow dancing
really is.

to every man
who ever asked me to slow-dance,
and every man who ever will

CONTENTS

TWO BY TWO

PROLOGUE

A Survivor's Tale

A typical dance/relationship story in this day and age, in two once happy lives. Starring Laurie Pepper, my cousin, and her ex-boyfriend, Hugh.

Laurie Pepper, my cousin, was once married to jazzman Art Pepper, which was a piece of cake, really, compared to her new boyfriend, Hugh, and their crazy dance history.

"When did you start dancing?" I asked.

"I just looked it up, I thought it was longer ago, but I only started dancing in September of nineteen ninety-two, and I did it because my boyfriend, Hugh, wanted to learn how to mambo. God, had I but known!"

"Well, didn't people warn you that it was bad for relationships if one of you was really great and the other was, uh, like Hugh?"

"Nobody warned me at all, or if they did, I didn't hear them, I just thought it would be *fun!*" Her voice is filled with rue.

"How many different kinds of anonymous programs did you have to practice to get through this?" I joked. (You know, like AA, Al-Anon, and Debtors Anonymous.)

"I would love to do an analysis of the amount of money I've spent, because we've joked about it and we've said it was about ten thousand dollars—but I don't think it's a joke, I think it might be more. On *private* lessons! It's not that expensive if you go to regular lessons, but unless you're really a good dancer to begin with . . . I had never danced at all in my whole life until, at the age of fifty-two, I went in to take dance lessons.

"So I went in as a complete novice, and if you do it that way, at that age, you cannot learn how to dance from group lessons. You just can't, I don't care what anyone says."

"That's why I always put 'free dance lessons' in quotes," I agree.

"Because what I wound up doing was buying a bunch of private lessons, and after a while I got so obsessed that my boyfriend and I couldn't dance together anymore because we were both so angry all the time."

"As I remember, you had to go to separate places, and he wouldn't go anywhere. And he was a terrible dancer."

"He was a *terrible* dancer—and I found a guy who would practice with me. That was kind of an issue too. I never went so far as to buy private lessons with an individual other than Hugh, but things really got very rocky for a couple of years!"

"Yeah," I remembered, "and then he left you for another dancer!"

"Well, that was the only place he went, so how could he meet anybody but a dancer? You should talk to him about that because he is really very witty. In the story he tells, well, we broke up and then he met this other woman very quickly. He said the only reason he was able to get her was that the sound system at Sportsman's Lodge went out and there was silence so he was able to talk to her. That's how he got his next girlfriend; he would never have scored otherwise, certainly not as a dancer."

"Why is it that we want to do these things at this age that we can't do and we take it personally when everyone's so mean to us?"

"Evie, that's an unanswerable question," my cousin said, as we laughed about this and poured out diet peach iced tea.

Thinking it over, she said, "Well, first of all everything changes. Everything changes about you—you eat differently, you dress differently, you think differently, and you assess people in terms of whether they can dance or not. Everything is geared toward the evening of dancing. And if you're really as insane as I think I was, you videotape every lesson so you can see how horrible you are!

"I used to videotape my practice sessions with Jerry. After two dances, we'd rewind the tape and look at ourselves, and we'd both moan. 'Oh, my shoulders, oh God, why don't I straighten my knee, oh, look at my feet, they're pointed out!' This was our entire conversation and then we'd get up and we'd try to do it again!"

"But you're both great dancers now," I mentioned, reminding her that Jerry had gone on to compete in salsa contests, and Laurie is fabulous—everyone loves dancing with her.

"I became a pretty good dancer; Jerry became an excellent dancer—that's the interesting thing. Hugh said it wouldn't hurt his feelings if you said he can't dance. But he *looks* like he can dance, because he's been asked by women to dance after they've seen him on the floor."

"Right," I said, "they don't know. But *I* like dancing with him, he's fun! Just because he's not on the two, what do I care?"

"Actually, when we went out on Friday, he danced *quite* well."

"He can dance the first three dances and then he gets tired, like me," I remind her, since I'm always leaving early, having gotten sated and tired. "So then you went to Pasadena Ballroom Dance?" I prompted.

"Yeah, because it was easier. First I went to Let's Dance L.A., with many private lessons with Anna and Marlon. Then Anna and Marlon went to Amsterdam, and I decided I wanted dancing to be fun. I hated it; I had had too many lessons from Renée and I had learned to hate myself—that's what you learn from Renée. I went to Pasadena Ballroom Dance because I wanted to learn the fox-trot and stuff, and at Let's Dance they didn't really concentrate on those things. So I went to Pasadena Ballroom Dance and I was a *star* there! I was a star because Renée had taught me how to follow and nobody else could follow."

"You weren't a star in Renée's eyes, but over there . . ."

"Over there I was a star and people would ask me where I'd been studying. I could give her the credit and say it was Renée, but I also began to enjoy it. Pasadena Ballroom changed my life because it made me feel like I was a good dancer, but the truth is that what's happened to me over time is that I don't like to go out dancing because I don't like dancing with drunks. I also don't like being criticized, but if I go to classes . . ."

"They don't criticize you in the fox-trot and cha-cha. They're perfectly nice!" I protested.

"But I don't like going out to clubs, I don't like waiting for someone to ask me to dance, so a class is much better. In a good class they'll rotate you every few minutes, you get a new partner. It's wonderful, absolutely wonderful—and the good dancers and bad dancers alike have to dance with you."

"Right, Paul McClure's classes are like that; in his workshops you'd dance with the good and bad dancers."

"In some classes they don't rotate you and it drives me mad, because all the good male dancers want to dance with either a really good dancer or a really beautiful young girl. That lets us out."

"Yeah, that's true," I concede, "zese men, zey are pigs. The two-step is not like that, though; everyone's very nice. So then you went to Pasadena, but you've never been to one of their dances."

"I've never been to one of their Saturday-night dances because I'm afraid nobody would ask me to dance."

"No, they're fun, because everybody asks everybody else to dance and everybody's in such a euphoric state. They have a snowball: they have four people at the beginning of the evening, four couples who, when the music stops after a few bars, pick out eight people to dance with. When the music stops again, those people pick out sixteen people to dance with. Pretty soon everybody in the whole room is doing this huge waltz, and after that everybody dances all the time. You dance every dance with everybody there, and pretty soon you wind up wringing wet and saying 'no, thank you.' "

"God, how great," she says. "But the only thing is, I can't dance West Coast Swing."

"But they don't do great West Coast Swing at Pasadena Ballroom Dance."

"I know, but they don't know that, they have a good time anyway."

"It's hard to follow them because their moves are, like, wrong!"

"I know, I know, but they don't care and they don't know. They're very out of it that way."

"I love the way they do East Coast Swing; I could do that forever there."

"They do jitterbug and lindy hop too. They don't want to get too good at West Coast Swing because they're the king of the lindy hop, that's the mystique. Everyone thinks they try to make West Coast Swing look bad so everybody will do the lindy hop instead."

"They succeed."

"I think they just don't know how to do it, it's not something you can just learn. It's really hard. It's harder than salsa."

"It's a philosophy," I agree.

"It's harder than salsa. Have you seen that woman who teaches at Let's Dance L.A.? That little blond woman, she's terrific."

"I know a lot of incredibly great West Coast dancers, but you know, it's got so much torque in it. Every time I take a lesson, my knees hurt—I think I'm too old," I said. "They sent me all this information, five pages, single-spaced on every page, and I want to put it in my book like that because it's so pedantic, like the dance itself. They're so crazy! They say it cannot be taught at Arthur Murray, and they must hate Pasadena Ballroom because of this, you know. So don't dance it over there, but they do everything else that's fun, they even have polkas."

"That's the one dance that I've done before that I know how to do." .

"Yeah, they do polkas! They do wonderful waltzes, and every-body gets pretty tired out. That's Hugh's secret too, he just gets tired like I do, and most people who aren't dancers get tired af-ter about an hour."

"Here's what happens to Hugh in the dance thing," Laurie said. "He goes out there and he's real nervous, so his first dance is not that great. By the end of the second dance, he's doing a lot better. The third dance is terrific, and the fourth dance is good. Then . . . that's it."

"Right, you have to practice for years and years and have in-credible stamina. Most people can hardly dance by ten-thirty," I said, "except for the professionals. Maurice is so terrifically on the money at midnight; by one or two o'clock A.M. he is totally into the music; every dance is to the music."

"I don't think Renée gets tired," Laurie supplied.

"But Maurice, if he walks two blocks he's out of breath," I said. "Dancing is not the same as aerobic exercise, it's stop and go. But anyway, I just figure that everything will work out okay."

"At Pasadena Ballroom Dance, I was an absolute star. During the breaks people would ask me to dance. Through that practice I learned all the dances, and I really loved it! Then my knee went."

"I think anytime I get near West Coast Swing, my knee goes. I think there's a voodoo torque in that dance."

"There's a lot of torque," Laurie, who just had a knee operation this year because of West Coast, agrees. "It's much harder on the knees than salsa, you're constantly rotating your legs."

"Right," I agree, "so you have to be under twenty-five to do it."

"Except that it's so much fun, and it's my favorite music. The thing was that Hugh loved Latin music. Latin music never possessed me the way Aretha, Ray Charles, or country music does. I mean, I could sing along to some of those songs forever."

"'Black Velvet,'" I agree, a great West Coast Swing song.

"There's this incredible record, Evie, I bought it 'cause Bobby used to use it, called *Taj Majal, Dancing to the Blues*. Bobby Cordoba would play it to the class, and nothing will get me down when that music is playing, I can't *not* dance. If I fuck up I don't care because the music is so wonderful. . . . Have you talked to Jerry lately?"

"Not for a long time. I heard that in his Phys Ed class in high school he's teaching dance class. He called me a couple of times, but I said, 'Oh, my knee, my knee, I'm waiting for my knee to get better,' and he gave up. I think he either stopped dancing or found another partner."

"His little Japanese girl is teaching salsa in Japan, and came in with Jerry for one or two lessons at Renée's, just to pick up some stuff."

"With her camcorder? She never says, 'Oh, my foot, oh, my shoulder, how horrible.' "

"Well, she hates herself equally."

"Oh, she does!"

"She hates herself in dance; to dance is to hate yourself."

"That's not true in two-step."

"It's true in salsa," she replies.

"It's true in salsa and tango, and it's true in West Coast Swing, but not as much because West Coast has that euphoria that comes from being counterweights. But the two-step is not about hating yourself at all, it's about modest good fun, ho, ho, ho."

"That's how Pasadena Ballroom Dance is!"

"That's right," I agree, "and that's why all the really fine teachers hate that place, because they say, 'Oh, you know, it's just a social thing.' And I'm wondering, do you want to get as good as they are so you can be *anti*social?"

"That, in a nutshell, is it. 'It's just a social thing.' I finally get it! What those people are doing is for competition purposes. Those people, they're like Olympic athletes, and they want to compete! They start out as gymnasts and ballet dancers or in clown school and things."

"You came to In Cahoots with me once for two-step."

"I did!" she remembered. "Yes, they asked me to dance; this guy just dragged me out to the floor and just taught me. . . . Now that's really, boy, that is so incredible, because if you went into any salsa place and a guy came over and asked you to dance and you said, 'I've never done this before,' he'd say, 'Oh, sorry' and go over and ask somebody else. But this guy, at In Cahoots, comes up to me, and I say I've never done it before, and he says, 'Well, you've come to the right place.' Then he takes me out on the floor and teaches me how and pretty soon, he was twirling me!"

"That's right," I remembered. "Were you doing the two-step?"

"Right, Texas two-step," she remembered, "and he really twirled me, did things I've never done before—backwards!"

"That's the easy one, that's why people like it."

"He started doing all sorts of tricks with me!"

"And you could follow."

" 'Cause I could follow! Because of Renée!"

"They have classes for doing turns right. Paul McClure's hands are great."

Laurie went back to thinking about salsa, and she remembered recently going into a Salsa Two class somewhere. "I was watching this guy who was really more advanced than Salsa Two, and he was just practicing. He had that snooty expression that they get, where they won't even look at you. They're just practicing their own form and if you can't do it, fuck you. But he led me, his touch was like a butterfly. It was wonderful. I followed, and I wondered what the hell he was doing with the other women who couldn't follow something like that. I could hardly feel his finger on me, but the direction with his finger told me everything that I needed to know. It's incredible how much information can be conveyed by a good dancer."

"Right, they don't break your arm either."

"Hugh is pretty good, until he gets tired and starts flinging you around a little too much. The thing I hate and I just have to . . . I just swore to myself that I wasn't going to criticize—I'd talk to him before . . ."

"You have to take a holy vow every time you go out with him."

"That's right, and it's because when he sends you out, he sends you out too far. He's got such long arms, and it's horrible because it takes forever to get back, and you only have a couple of beats. I just swore that I wouldn't mind and I didn't."

Anyway, I was trying to convince Laurie to come with me one night to Pasadena Ballroom Dance, and I described one of the great male dancers there who, though he'd rather be doing West

Coast at The Crest, did condescend to come to these dances in Pasadena. When I danced a fox-trot with him, *nothing* was more of a thrill or an adventure; he just plowed forward with such a great glee and vengeance.

"The fox-trot is not about anything but moving to the music in a beautiful way," I remind her, "and it hardly throws your knees out at all. That's why I like Maurice."

"It's a lost art, smooth dances," Laurie agreed. "I loved dancing West Coast to that music. Oh, my knee, my knee!"

"You must tell everyone they should take ballroom before they take salsa or tango or West Coast Swing"—I want to remind myself, and Laurie wants to remind people too. "So they can learn how to follow."

"You must learn how to follow," Laurie says, "so you can learn how to dance. But the one thing about learning on those hard dances is that even though it nearly kills you, destroys your relationships, your life, your morale, makes you hate yourself, changes your philosophy into something really scurrilous and stinking . . . even though it does all those things—when you finally do one of those other dances, those easy ballroom dances, you are a god, you are a *god* on the dance floor! That's what happens!"

"Right. And there's no such thing as a 'free' dance class."

Hugh has a new hobby, reading Proust. It's much more in his vein, since brilliance, wit, repartee, and the spoken word are his métier, not Latin dancing.

1

Fox-Trot with the Fabulous
Johnny Crawford Band

I don't understand the fox-trot," my friend Kassie told me in the ladies' room of the Atlas. "I just don't get it."

Since Kassie got *all* other dances, from West Coast Swing to tango, the Hustle, salsa, the milonga, even the waltz, and East Coast Swing, and got them so well that all the men just came flying out of the woodwork to dance with her (when with me it was like pulling teeth back then to get them to do *anything*), I thought, "Well, I *do* sort of understand the fox-trot." I mean, it's practically the only dance I *do* understand.

I mean, what's not to understand about Frank Sinatra songs or Glenn Miller?

I was lucky because right then I was formally introduced to Maurice Schwartzman, who was sitting at our table the first night I went to see the 1928 Johnny Crawford Society Dance Orchestra. The table was made up of the aforementioned Kassie McConnel, Jim Hines, who had been her partner for so long, Doz, who was a new friend of theirs because she loved tango so much, and the Great Maurice: a man I'd seen before, not only dancing in movies, dressed as a diplomat or something with this soigné goatee, but also in real life. A few years ago Orlando Paiva was teaching tango at the Studio for Performing Arts (in West Hollywood) and Maurice refused to practice the step with me on the grounds that he wasn't there.

"You're not *here*?" I wondered.

"No," he said, "I'm not in this class, I'm only here to pick up a few pointers."

And with that, he picked up this twenty-year-old girl who was a great dancer on top of everything, unlike me, and left. But of course, I'd been in the dance scene long enough to know being witty gets you nowhere. Just because I could once get a great table at Elaine's or in certain social settings I am considered an asset, in the tango world, if they don't think you *are* somebody, and unless you can really dance, forget it.

Later, I saw him again at Norah's. At first I thought he was Leonard Bernstein or something, he entered with such an air of grandiosity you'd think he was about to conduct the New York Philharmonic in a cape. But instead, that night rather than dance the tango, he danced salsa with this woman and I thought, "This guy, not only is he into clothes worse than anyone, but he can *dance*."

Anyway, the woman he was with that night had never looked so great doing the cha-cha before. When I heard later that Madonna danced salsa with him at Norah's, I wasn't surprised, because he looked like he knew everybody, had been everywhere, and would do anything—provided it didn't mean he had to be "here" if he didn't want to dance with you.

I couldn't believe that Kassie had actually managed to convince Maurice that I was such a famous author and such a glory to the community that he practically kissed my hand. And I don't know how Kassie did this because under no circumstances had she or would she ever read a book, but since my "Tangoland" story had appeared in my last collection of short stories, I finally had cachet and people actually were nice to me—way beyond my danceworthiness. Which was good, because I had no danceworthiness, and in fact my only aspiration now was that I wouldn't mind learning easy dances, ballroom types, like the fox-trot for example. (At least, if you got stuck in a bar in Hong Kong with a combo and some mysterious stranger asked you to dance, it would probably be a fox-trot.)

Anyway, I couldn't believe that this Maurice was actually there at our table, being happy to meet me. Later on I would hear women say, "That Maurice, he's impossible. Just impossible. Except for smooth dances. On those, he's the best." The fox-trot is the ultimate smooth dance.

From the moment we all clapped eyes on Johnny Crawford and his amazing band, we were dazzled. He turned everything into either the decadent twenties, when the Charleston was king, or the sad thirties, when everyone was too depressed to Charleston anymore and Fred and Ginger took the fox-trot to amazingly smooth lengths.

Johnny Crawford is the same Johnny Crawford who was a little boy on *The Rifleman*, a series everybody but me had seen. Now that he was grown up, he'd become an incredible fount of musical knowledge of the twenties and thirties, conducting a great band with musical scores straight out of that time period. He wore a top hat and tuxedo, and could actually sing these great old songs, sounding like he was coming from long ago, from the radio high atop the Rainbow Room in New York City.

And the Atlas was a nightclub that was just like Greta Garbo, who a writer once said looked like other women after two drinks. The Atlas looked like other nightclubs after two drinks— it was heavenly, elegant, beautiful, like being inside a movie about crossing the Atlantic in a ritzy steamer. In fact, part of Johnny Crawford's mystique was that between sets, old movies would appear on a screen behind the orchestra stand, and you could dance "inside" them—inside Busby Berkeley numbers, inside Dietrich's gorilla routine or rarely seen footage of great old dancers doing amazing stuff.

Or you *would* be able to dance inside these things, if Maurice could be persuaded to dance with you. He wouldn't do this if anyone respectable were looking, or unless Miranda Garrison, the great dancer-choreographer and his good friend, was there, in which case nothing would stop either of them from dancing four hours straight.

It was here and then that I learned what the word "smooth" meant.

"Your shoulders, what's the matter with you!" Maurice would say, at first trying to lead me. "How can I lead you if you move like *that?*"

It was here, having this great band to dance to, that I learned how to move so smoothly that Maurice could hardly complain at all. It was here that I learned to just loosen myself into fox-trot, which, to me, is the world's most logical dance because it is danced to the most beautiful songs. Just like Fred and Ginger, except Maurice never expected us to suddenly dance on tables. It was all smooth and all shoulders held steady, all grace, and practically all effortless. It was surprisingly fast and then wrapped in twirls and arms, and then stops, and then back to the dance once more.

Everybody else was dying to do the only two tangos that Johnny would play with Maurice because his tangos were just incredible. But for me, having already had my fill of tango and knowing I'd never be good, much less great, I was happy just to do fox-trots. Luckily, the wonderful Miranda Garrison, who loved doing fox-trots with him, too, was often out of town choreographing movies.

The whole essence of the fox-trot is that it's a dance where women are supposed to be elegant and smooth, dancing to a time I could actually feel in my soul is exactly what someone as big and otherwise clumsy as me could look okay doing. Everyone I knew in the dance world was incredibly tiny; at best I was a size 12—the largest you can be and still fit into mediums at the store. Everyone in the dance world is a small.

All the other dances like salsa or West Coast, you have to be a genius with years of private lessons to do at all well. But dancing a fox-trot with Maurice was like getting vast experience for free, learning to float. Floating is not a feeling I often experience in dancing, except with Maurice.

We all went nuts at the Atlas, all the women who loved dancing, getting dressed in more and more outrageous costumes. We all wound up with these incredible earrings from Michael Morrison, which were basically designed so Las Vegas showgirls could stand at the top of a stairway and be visible from a block away; these things dangling off their ears, four inches long, made of Austrian crystal glued to cork, so they wouldn't be so heavy that your ears hurt. I had about ten pairs of these earrings. The Atlas was so dimly lit, you needed to glow in the dark.

Kassie began dressing like a Jean Cocteau extra from some unreal movie with silver leaves glued to her chiffon midriff. Sometimes she was the World's Most Glamorous Movie Star, with clinging white dresses that had long fringe. We all went overboard into bangles, lipstick, gilded headbands, diamond chokers—the works.

I wound up with a Hanna Hartnell (a local designer who's a friend of mine) silk taffeta skirt that had been hand-dyed in Hong Kong to be both black and red. It was opalescent like something amazing from some Paris opera gown, and crisp to do fox-trots in. I wore it with a black clingy top, low-cut.

Cute Steve, the guy who was then managing the Atlas, got so into it all that he actually printed a newsletter with pictures of Kassie and her outfits on the cover. It all just completely overtook us and we were all, each week, just dying for Thursday night to come again, so we could go back to the Atlas in ever increasingly bedazzling outfits and wow each other. Maurice, of course, had better clothes than anybody—white linen suits. He looked liked an Henri Lartigue photograph from 1920, only more dangerous.

As time went by, the only people who ever ate dinner were Jim and Kassie. This, naturally, was not that great a thing for the Atlas, which survived on serving great food, not pandering to dancers getting all dressed up in boas and sequins and earrings from *The Day the Earth Stood Still*. They began having a $10 cover charge, which for a lot of people was too much, so fewer and fewer could afford to come.

I would spend four hours there with Maurice, doing these unbelievable fox-trots, and not have a single thing except iced tea. I was having way too much fun to eat, and got down for a while to a size 10.

The amazing thing was, Maurice lived near me. In the dance world this was astounding because most people you dance with have to drive miles on the freeway to get anywhere. It turned out that except for Wednesdays and Saturdays, Maurice went dancing every night—all over the place, high and low.

Every so often, Maurice would take me to these places with him. Senior citizens' centers were really fun. They'd get these live bands to play old-style sambas, cha-chas, and stuff like that, at a Masonic temple where there was this huge dance floor. Then all these unbelievable ladies in their seventies and eighties, who were incredible dancers, would float around in spiked heels like dainty spiders.

We went to the Derby, but Maurice hated it because the floor was too small. Occasionally we'd meet at El Floridita on a Monday night when they had this great Johnny Polenca band. Renée Victor sometimes went, scaring the "Mambo Society" faction with her mambo that was way better than they ever dreamed of. I thought it was hilarious that people who were extras in *The Mambo Kings* actually had the pretension to call themselves the Mambo Society, like they were in charge of the mambo and everyone else was nobody. They'd actually tell men who didn't dance on the "two" that they "couldn't dance," which set up a schism between the older dancers and the younger ones with fire and beauty.

At El Floridita, if the floor wasn't jammed, Maurice would attempt to do salsa with me, but this is not a dance I'm made for. I prefer slow cha-chas, and he did salsa so fast, you had to be a genius to keep up with him.

Sometimes we'd go to the Beverly Hills Arthur Murray, where on some Saturday nights, they'd have these "dances." One after another, you'd be able to do the rumba, the cha-cha, the fox-trot, even the tango and merengue and everything, on this floor that was totally unbelievable because you could do no wrong smooth dancing on it, whereas the Atlas's floor was cement.

When Maurice started dancing, he was nineteen years old and had gone back to Canada from the Pratt Institute in New York (where he was studying to be an architect). He had gone to a dance in New York and there saw that the most sought-after and popular men were not ones with good character or virtue, but those who could lead. He felt this wasn't fair, though in Canada he got a summer job at Arthur Murray, where they not only taught him to dance, but how to teach, and he won a national contest of all Arthur Murray teachers, being the best in dance on earth. Which in my humble opinion, he still might be—though his character could, of course, have gone downhill since now that he can dance, he doesn't need any.

For five years, when he was first starting out in his own business, he actually didn't dance at all. He just kept his nose to the grindstone and from this his business flourished, enough so that when he wasn't doing it, he was out dancing as much as possible, often getting parts in movies as a dance extra.

Today he is a retired businessman, but a lot of his life is spent dancing. He gets parts in commercials, he is a dance extra in movies, and Robert Duvall is one of his closest friends. This enabled him to take a picture of himself strangling Adolf Eichmann, because Duvall played him in a movie and said it was okay. Maurice, the son of a rabbi and a refugee from Hitler, takes the Third Reich war criminals personally. Being half Jewish myself, I take them personally too, but it never would have occurred to me to ask Duvall to let me strangle him in his Eichmann makeup.

Robert Duvall always calls Maurice up whenever he's coming to town, so Maurice can tell him where all the hot dance action is. Duvall is smart; he's even learning salsa better. Renée said, "He's improved, but he won't admit it. That shows a real dancer; they never tell you how great they are! On this last movie we were on together, in Louisiana, we went out Cajun dancing every night. What a blast."

There are some places Robert Duvall cannot go because he'll be mobbed, but at dance places, maybe everyone's so intent on the music, the night, and their partner, they don't mind a movie star there doing the same thing.

In the dance world in L.A., Maurice knows everyone. He knows the old owner of Myron's Ballroom (it also used to be a disco, Vertigo's, in the eighties), which is now called Grand Street and does salsa. Maurice took me there a couple of times, but really the place is too far away and too cold, if you ask me. I do love the decor, though, and the fact that underneath the floor, there are springs so people can dance all night and not hurt their feet.

Back in the olden days of Los Angeles, the Alexandria Hotel, which is still downtown though now a drug-dealing spot, was the greatest dance floor for all the movie stars. Rudolph Valentino danced there with Mae Murray (who fittingly described herself as "the self-enchanted"—the title of her autobiography). Then the Biltmore Hotel opened up with its various ballrooms and it had the best hotel band to broadcast out of there live, from 1927 to 1932 or something, or at least so Johnny Crawford has told me.

Johnny Crawford is even more of an L.A. maniac than I am, entangling his historical knowledge with music scores and which bands played where. The fact that his band moved from the Atlas over to the Biltmore Hotel and now call themselves the Biltmore Band is completely in keeping with an obsession people like us have—the desire to keep people from tearing L.A. apart totally so some of it will still be standing when the earthquake comes and sweeps us into some new configuration.

Even though it's now farther away from where I live, I still love going to the Biltmore. It was there, when I was fourteen years old, that I began my faux "modeling" career. A father of one of my father's violin students was in the garment industry, a seller of "schmattas" to department stores. Twice a year they had these big shows in the upstairs hotel rooms of the Biltmore, and I got to go downtown and pretend I was a model—just as my benefactor pretended he didn't mind the schmatta business. But he was lucky because his sister, Bess Cooper, was the biggest buyer at the May Company and would buy all his stuff without him having to try too hard.

To me the Biltmore was the height of glamour. The inside

lobby was incredible, and being able to think of myself as a model (I was a size 12, but nobody cared, it was just for fun) helped, since growing up actually *in* Hollywood can definitely make you worry that you're not Tina Louise.

At the Biltmore, in fact, one of those times, the great Bess Cooper came in just as I was berating a midwestern lady buyer for not buying enough of these things made of fake fur with a knit collar. I just knew all the girls would want it because it made you look cute, wholesome, and huggable, like a teddy bear with a girl's head. It was called a "pooh-bear."

"You mean because *you* don't like them," I told her, "no girls will be able to *buy* them? How *mean!*"

The lady walked out, having reluctantly ordered maybe half a dozen.

Bess figured I was a fourteen-year-old who must be in the know, and she ordered 8 zillion. Thus she put the company out of business because they couldn't fill the orders fast enough, though the ones they did put in the May Company sold like hotcakes and all the girls were pining for more. The one I got I wore, and wore, and loved.

From then on, Bess Cooper invited me to come with her when she went buying at the Biltmore for the teenage girl department, which could have turned into a job for me, if I hadn't already decided to be a writer or artist.

So today, whenever I enter the Biltmore's beautiful lobby and head into the glittery hallway where the Crystal Room is (where the old band used to do radio shows), it's as if I've stepped back into my own history. Now it's amazing to see the Johnny Crawford's wonderful Biltmore Band, and the whole room is seething with Old L.A. mystique. Johnny, his wife, and I all graduated from Hollywood High and wish it were the fifties again, when the mustard trees, the old Schwab's, all that were still here.

Kassie followed Johnny Crawford to the Biltmore. She arrives even more beautiful now than before (she's always more beautiful than before, it's part of her Art), and for a while, we were all wearing the amazing boas, but they shed so much, it looked like colorful birds had been killed on the dance floor.

Sometimes the lindy hoppers show up nowadays, the swing dancers who are totally great and amazingly bedecked, and luckily, there's enough room on the floor for everyone. This one couple, Jeff and Denise, come in amazing clothes and dance an amazing dance called the Balboa.

It's great to have Maurice living not too far from me because sometimes when he's not busy with his incredibly high-society, movie-star social life, he comes with me to dances at Pasadena Ballroom. He loves dancing with Erin, and she's one of the few women who doesn't think he dances fast dances too fast. When they play fox-trots, we can do them on the huge church dance floor, sweeping around the whole room, dissolving and returning, twirls and whirls, me, Maurice, and those great old songs with the great old lyrics. It's heavenly—in a church with the sisters of Pasadena whose premise is fun.

Of course, heaven with Maurice is problematic because of one thing people hate about him. At the end of the evening, he's still dancing as correctly, as in time, and as beautifully as at the beginning. Most men give out and by ten or so are just phoning it in. Maurice always gives each dance he's doing a hundred percent of what the dance is about. He's an artist.

Every so often, people decide they have to take "private lessons" with him. He's told several that he's $300 an hour, but this didn't stop one couple who insisted he teach them both to at least do a waltz for their wedding. Recently he suddenly decided he might go down to $150 and build up a clientele among the very rich, because dancing is coming back so much he's always hounded.

Marie France, who danced in the American Ballet Theater for ten years and even danced with Baryshnikov, told me, "Maurice is a natural in ballroom dancing. He doesn't follow sets, he creates in the moment, which is amazing. He just lets the music move him through the floor."

What I've learned in all this time of dancing is that people who dance have a lot—if not better lives, at least better clothes. Plus we can fit into clothes we wore long ago in high school, whereas most people our age have a terrible time staying trim. Not to mention, if you're dancing with the opposite sex, you want to look cute. For me that's always a reason not to eat that fried chicken, dessert, whatever—because it'll be more fun to wear that Hanna Hartnell taffeta skirt, the skirt of the forever fox-trot of the gods.

2

Two-Step with Paul McClure

The first time I saw Paul teach, it was a *thrill*," Jim said. "He's just such an intellectual."

I don't know about much, but for me, if it hadn't been for Paul McClure adding little extras, like "If you don't know the step just ignore those who do, you're more creative anyway," I don't think I could have become so charmed by and had as much fun in the In Cahoots world as I do. Because, though it's very beautiful to watch the dancers and all, I don't think I would have felt at home without Paul there—classing the joint up, being the intellectual, a fish out of water like me.

I don't know about you, but there are some people there who intimidate me. Often they are Scorsese wise-guy types, or Cal Tech Intellectuals, computer programmers, people who work in banks—all of whom take just one look at that two-step, and suddenly their life is cowboy kerchiefs and getting boots to fit just right. From then on, they *know* where their social life is going to be. From then on, it's quick-quick/slow-slow, forever and ever, Amen.

And I don't know about you, but isn't country music getting amazing? Wynonna, all these great women, and the guys, Clint Black? All those charming men in hats? *Aren't* they cute? Country music seems the only stuff in America with *lyrics* anymore. (All the stuff kids like, it's too busy and important to pander to people like me who want to know "What did they say, what did they say?")

43

Luckily enough when I wanted to learn the dance, I went to In Cahoots, this Dallas saloon chain in Glendale, not too far from my house. The first night I saw Paul McClure with his cowboy hat, his cowboy boots, his Wrangler jeans (they only wear Wranglers and they have to come from Sears), and his charming western accent. He was leading a class of beginners, maybe seventy people—some of whom had never done *anything* before, never danced with a partner before—and now here he was trying to teach men to lead and women to follow.

Following is such a weird concept anyway, women mirroring what men want, *exactly*—trying not to be a hindrance, not to drag them down.

In America today, what's happening between men and women has gotten so ridiculous. The waivers the kids going to Oberlin College have to sign so they know whether they're "date raped" or not; the methods men employ to get girls, importing wives from poverty-stricken countries. I mean, I know why men are so desperate, but they don't have to be. All they have to be is a so-so two-step dancer, and they'll at least have American women asking them to dance.

Paul McClure starts from scratch, teaching at this very beginner level "free" two-step class: how men should touch women, how softly their hands should take their partner's, how careful they should be not to wreck her hair, her outfit, her upper torso. The two-step, the way it is in Glendale nowadays, it may be a country dance but it's from a country where women wear modest clothes, don't want to be touched, and basically, though they're dancing, have not surrendered one iota of dignity.

There used to be a great two-step place in western L.A., Denim and Diamonds. People loved this place but somehow it recently closed (probably because dancers don't eat anything, don't drink anything but water, and don't want to spend any money), so all the great dancers now go to In Cahoots in Glendale. The parking lot there, which has valet parking on weekends, is crammed with Jeeps, Mercedeses, Lexuses, Corvettes, four-wheel-drive vehicles, the works—people who come to Glendale only because of the two-step.

My old boyfriend from when I was in junior high, Louie, loved Denim and Diamonds so much, he desperately tried to learn the two-step for two whole years. Alas, he never quite made it—even though he has the look of Joey Buttafuoco and the rap sheet, practically, to match, he wanted to be a cowboy, or a faux cowboy anyway.

Real cowboys, their boots are too hard to dance in if you ask me.

Like a lot of people who fell under the two-step spell before I realized the tricks, I bought these real cowboy boots from a fancy cowboy boot store, before I realized, these boots are made for riding horses, not *dancing.* The kind of boots the dancers use are called Evenin' Stars; they're sold either at country dancing competitions or in L.A. Anyway, you can call this guy, Dennis, who will bring you these boots for $160. If you're wearing panty hose, you can yank these boots over your feet and from then on, you never have to worry about your feet again.

"I've got twelve pairs," one woman told me. "They are *so* great, they feel like—I don't know—dancing on air."

If you wear real cowboy boots and take a step, your heel will usually slip out of your boot, because this is necessary for getting onto a horse. If you wear Evenin' Stars, horses are the furthest thing from your mind; being able to move very fast with absolute precision is the only thing you care about.

"They were invented by this company for contest dancers," the guy who sold them to me told me. "Country dancers were not allowed to wear jazz boots, you know, by Capezio, which everyone wanted to wear, but the judges wouldn't allow it, it wasn't 'country.' So this place, they invented boots that fit like jazz boots but look like cowboy boots; the soles are suede, the lining is nylon; they're very light, not like cowboy boots at all—and they *fit*."

Of course, talking about feet is boring, but most dancers get all animated when they tell you how great their shoes are, who makes the best shoes, where they got certain shoes. But the happiest are two-steppers with Evenin' Stars, because with those shoes, dancing all night is just a breeze and you wake up the next day with just feet, rather than swollen-in-pain stumps. Well gee, no wonder Evenin' Stars are so popular—and worth every penny.

Oh, thank you, God, for my Evenin' Stars, and for Paul McClure, who hangs around after and before class, willing to impart these vital pieces of information to people complaining their boots are falling off.

Unlike most teachers, Paul McClure is so into it for the "social" part of "social dancing" that he actually dances with beginners who can't dance a lick, he just likes it all so much. Unlike most teachers, he dances with people he's never met before, and he doesn't try to browbeat them, he just lets everyone move at their own pace.

He looks like a mixture of Harrison Ford and Paul Newman in *Hud*, but he has an easygoing persona, allowing beginners to just hang in there. On the weekends, he teaches "workshops" all around town—$10 for two hours—and in those, you can really get better, because you dance with so many people and it's just so much fun. He's written a book called *Cowboy Etiquette*—or his alter ego, "Pablo," has written it. He's such a double Pisces, he's got this entire double life going—by day he's a Doctor of Business Management, teaching in local colleges to people seeking progress in real life, and by night, he's the two-step teacher at In Cahoots and a place in San Dimus, The Western Connection. In June, he had instigated a country dance festival in Riverside, and it was there that I first took pictures of people dancing, during a Jack and Jill West Coast Swing contest. There I was dazzled by these adorable and charming people, just having as much fun as they could, under his transcendent aura of Intellectual Country Dance Charm.

He attracts coeds from Cal Tech like Kristin, getting her doctorate in robotic engineering, people who live in their minds and need a place to go have fun that's filled with energy and silliness. In his mind, the two-step done well is a feat of mathematical precision, because if you don't swim like a fish, you'll have trouble.

In spite of *Urban Cowboy* portraying a really great but mean dancer, it's hard to imagine a really great two-step dancer who would be mean; the dance is so antithetical to that vibe. The places these people dance are very friendly; it's not cool to be mean, it's not "country."

One of the reasons country stars are so popular—right now, anyway—is that so many Americans are sick of no manners, bad attitudes, grudging behavior, violence, O. J. Simpson's trial, and Bill Clinton's impeachment, they had to find something left in America that still seems sane—and country is sane. The stars better stay sane, too, because if they "go Hollywood," country fans glaze over and think, "Now wait a minute; I thought this guy was one of us. Now he's dumped his wife, his manager, his Wranglers! What is this? Why would I buy *his* record?"

I remember the first country star I loved, Johnny Cash. His "I Walk the Line" came out when I was in junior high or high school. It just touched me, because his voice was so personal and so sad: "I keep my eyes wide open all the time, because you're mine, I walk the line." Back in those days, the popular songs were all either goopy or else it was Ray Charles. Nobody spoke for guys who had been to jail and wanted to go straight for love.

Driving to In Cahoots on a Tuesday around 6:00 P.M. (the class begins at 6:30), I pass Brand Avenue with all the car dealers, Forest Lawn (such an inspiration to Evelyn Waugh), and plenty of Armenian kabob shops, along with a little flower shop called the Honey Bee. The Honey Bee seems left over from the James M. Cain days, when Mildred Pierce lived in Glendale and her husband left her. To make ends meet she sold pies, working so hard she turned a food stand into a chain, moved to Pasadena, and eventually wound up as Joan Crawford and got an Oscar—imagine, a girl from Glendale.

Glendale is the most American of L.A.'s cities; it's chipper and cheerful, it's optimistic and sweet. Unfortunately, it's also the home of the American Nazi Party, but they had to move somewhere, and Glendale is so sweet, maybe it's just that they had good taste.

Being Jewish myself, I have always felt Glendale needed a deli at least, and it did recently get one but not a very good one. They've got better Italian delis there, but then, since I've begun dancing, the whole look of Glendale has changed for me. I've decided that, well, maybe to attract the best dancers, there had to be a place that is outside of Hollywood and the west side enough for people to concentrate and practice. To picture Glendale, think of Debbie Reynolds's character in the movie *Singin' in the Rain*—nonblond hair, but a great voice, and a great dancer. She was just a teenager and had won Miss Burbank, which is Glendale-adjacent. Also, it was in a Glendale backyard that Margot Kidder was found—two days after landing at LAX, thirty miles from Glendale—after disappearing during a manic-depressive episode. It's not like she wound up in South Central, it was only Glendale, even if she had no teeth and no clothes. There's even a Disney branch in Glendale, the "Imagineering" section, where they invent the rides and do all the computer graphics for the parks.

Anyway, I try to come around 6:15 so I can warm up and admire whatever Paul and his dance partner, Lee, are wearing lately. I love In Cahoots because it's such a cowboy scene. You enter In Cahoots through old-timey saloon doors and it's got pool tables, that serious smoking-and-drinking smell, dark walls with Tanya Tucker posters. Then you walk down a dark, long walkway, attracted by the music and light of the dance floor, which even has those colored lights from a crystal chandelier-style thing. By this time, I'm totally pumped up because I love bars, I love music, and I love dance floors. I used to just *live* at a place somewhat like this, the Troubadour Bar, back in the days when I was a twenty-five-year-old groupie, trying to get into Glenn Frey's life.

Derek, who's new, took his first lesson with Paul at the Saturday workshop. Because he'd never danced before, or at least not with a partner, he was still at the look-at-his-feet stage. Dancing was almost beyond him, but he was so inexperienced, he didn't know. And people in country have to be nice because if you're not, you're not country.

"It's hard to catch on, because at the class there were too many guys, so I had to sit out dances and it's hard to catch on without practice."

Derek is thirty. "I've only liked country music for a little over a year, from listening to the radio—KZLA is my favorite station."

In the class, as Paul begins, there are about fifteen couples, maybe a few more. Each class begins with the men first, circling the dance floor, going quick-quick/slow-slow—short-

short/long-long—trying to get them to get the feet movement. If you've done other partner dancing before this is pretty easy, it's what's called a "smooth dance" (it's a fox-trot), and smooth dances have gliding steps.

"You keep your head up, left, right, left, right."

He then makes the ladies do what the guys did, backward, his voice always patient yet clear.

What was hard for me, and still is, is doing the half turns in time, though when they're done that way, people look like they're walking on water and when they're not, you look raggedy and inept.

From the very first lesson, he tries to instill the dance position where it's easiest for men to lead, i.e., the woman keeps a slightly backward lean in the man's right hand. This is the look of Viennese waltzers and when really good two-steppers dance this way, the torque is so fabulous, it looks *easy.* Though for me after all that tango and salsa when you're not supposed to be rigid, it's quite a shock. However, without a flat back none of the great turns can be led, and if you can't do the great turns, you have no fun.

Because it's a country dance, in the two-step the upper body is chaste—and the flatter your back, the more chaste you can appear; modesty itself. There is so much to remember when doing this dance; it's no wonder it usually takes people longer to learn it than they thought it should, especially if they've never danced before.

"This isn't high school, where you lean together in slow dances," he explains. "In this one, you have to lean back, ladies, to be together as a unit."

The beginner lesson, just learning to go quick-quick/slow-slow, takes about five or six minutes. Then he moves on to the intermediate lesson, which usually involves the girls doing turns, going into "sweetheart position," and usually these are moves Paul just invents out of whole cloth because his mind is too busy for just teaching easy stuff.

He explains all the things that facilitate dancing the strict line of dance that the two-step requires, the total commitment by everyone at a modern two-step place to understand, you move forward, you *always* move, and you never stop or go backward. My nightmare for two-step is falling down in front of the Valkyrie Ice Skaters and looking like a freeway pileup or a football accident.

What the two-step lacks in schmaltzy expressionism it makes up for in *speed* and almost miraculous arm turns, holds, spins, and so on that you can in no other dance do with such conviction that you're not going to plow into anyone or get plowed into. A nice change for a dance floor.

Of all the partner dancing, the two-step is the most comfortable, in that everyone's wearing flats (or Evenin' Stars), the clothes are not too fancy, and even not denim is a necessity.

In Paul's classes a lot of people who are in it only for the fun frequently come back week after week—partly to take the intermediate class, which begins at 7:30, but also to be under the spell cast by Paul himself, which is so country and sweet, yet so literate, so elegantly spoken.

He always, if given half a chance, makes jokes. Unlike a lot of teachers, who use the bad-cop sledgehammer style of teaching, Paul's unkind words are never for you, but only for himself. If you do the step wrong, he instantly apologizes for telling it to you wrong. His entire aura is of Merlin-like enchantment. When he's there, there are no bad manners, there is nothing coarse, nothing unprofessional.

Even the very first time, you get that feeling of the entire dance floor filled with oncoming traffic, of which you are an integral part. It's really a thrill and it needs someone like Paul, the intellectual cowboy, to keep everyone at their best, and yet transcendently in bliss.

In one of the first weeks I met Paul McClure, he agreed to let me interview him and we went to this restaurant in Glendale, Conrad's (a suspiciously Glendale-type name).

"The folks are so nice," he says about In Cahoots, "and once you get acquainted, it's just like the Cheers bar, everybody knows your name."

"I've seen a lot of dance places where people are mean."

"In ballroom competitions, people cut each other off the floor, the competition is cutthroat. For goodness' sake, that's nine to five, you don't have to do that on your own time."

"That's true." I laugh.

"I wonder if in something cute and friendly like two-step, it attracts a different kind of person."

"Or if the dance makes them that way?" I wondered too. "Maybe the restrictions of the dancing just drive the ballroom people crazy."

"I never thought about that."

"You know, I used to hate West Coast Swing, but now that I've seen it, I really love it."

"You know, it's so awesome. When someone dances well, it's a pleasure to dance with them, it's a pleasure to watch them. A good dance where you're both *on*—nothing feels better than that dance. And when you're really grooving together, you feel the music, the beauty, the partnership, the sensuality. . . ."

"So how old were you when you started dancing?" I wondered then.

"Forty-five."

"What sign are you?" I asked.

"Pisces," he said.

"The dance sign!" I said. "The sign of rose-colored glasses."

"Well, that fits."

Paul's chocolate malt arrives and he orders a wheat toast, while I order a waffle and bananas (that was before I got on the Zone diet and lost twenty-five pounds on pistachio ice cream).

"Pisces is also the sign of the ballet, gauze, compassion, and forgiveness."

"That seems to fit; I never put much stock in astrology. But I never did much dancing except for slow dancing in high school."

"That was fun?"

"Was it ever! But then I did nothing. The problem was, when I was younger I used to be pretty smart. I'm not smart anymore."

"You've outgrown it?" I wondered.

"I started in school early. I was always the youngest in my class by at least a year. I was a little skinny kid, which made it even worse—I got good scholarship grades but bad citizenship grades 'cause of the maturity issue. So I was always on an academic track, and because I was smaller and younger, never did anything physical. I had no clue that I had any kind of physical ability at all, any kind of athletic capability. Then I came into dancing, and when I started dancing I didn't have any ability there either, because I had never done it. I was trying to find a girlfriend."

"You?" I couldn't believe it, but by then he was on his second divorce, having had three children.

"I was going to this office party. It seemed I was the only person in there who didn't have a cowboy hat and jeans and have the look, and of course I couldn't dance, but the wives of some of the guys were patient and coached me through a few steps. I could see that this was a ton of fun. So the next Monday, I called the City of Hemmet, where I was living, and asked if there were lessons anywhere in town and they said, 'Sure, at the recreation center tonight.'

"So I went that night to a line dance lesson and started there. I wasn't good to start with, but then I hung in there and got better and more comfortable and started dancing on a performance team, and then began competing as a couple."

"So you had an ordinary life before this?"

"Yes, I got married first when I was twenty, had my first kid at twenty-two, and I was in college going through to a Ph.D."

"Well, this kind of dancing is so straight."

"Well, this is kind of good-mannered, good protocol."

I burst into my tango story, ending with inviting him to come to one of the tango evenings in a few weeks where Orlando would be and I say, "Well, half the people probably won't speak to each other there."

"That happens with competition couples. They're there learning their moves, they don't know enough to analyze them and fix them yet. Back in Nashville they had the World Championship, there's all kinds of divisions, age divisions, and so . . ."

"The couple who won looked dazed; they'd only danced together seven months."

"Well, they should look dazed if they'd only danced together seven months. Their routines are so complex."

I look across Conrad's Diner; the wonderful Paul McClure is sitting there, about to embark on a career as an impresario—his second annual Riverside Country Dance Festival. And here he is, someone who majored in business.

"What are you doing? You know you can't make any money out of dancing!" I point out.

"You're right. For one thing you can't copyright the dance moves. You can patent a mechanical device for other kinds of things, but here, you invent something and it belongs to the world. So, if you're looking to money, keep on looking. It's not in dancing."

"All the people I know who are into dancing, most of them have daily lives; they are lawyers or in business or computers."

"If you talk to people, at least at In Cahoots, who dance and dance well, they almost all have kind of analytical jobs. Because you think about dance, with the choreography and the movement, it's fairly complex, it's three-dimensional, it's moving down the floor, it's going in and out of traffic! Because of all the surprises that occur, you have to be able to adapt instantly, it's really complex. You could take a really smart person and they can lie awake at night trying to think how all these pieces fit together and keep themselves entertained for hours."

"Wow!"

"So dancing isn't for dummies," he ended.

"But don't you find people who are idiots savants, great dancers but just really terrible at other things: physical geniuses?"

"Actually, not too many. The ones who get into that are usually the ones who started dancing early. It kept them away from more lucrative occupations because it's like being a musician or a poet: you discover this talent early and you get all these people saying, 'I'm going to play the trumpet for a living.' Well, you're not going to make much of a living! So, you know, these bright people are highly motivated and are balked in an area like that where their talent has really put them in a rathole. That happens with people who have danced really early and become dance teachers rather than having a backup occupation. I like the tradition of having two occupations where there's something to fall back on.

"In the old days the band had to hide behind the chicken wire so the beer bottles wouldn't hit them, but those days are gone. The dancing (if you want to call it that) that went on then, wasn't really dancing like this, it was just starting out and leaning against your partner and hoping you weren't drunk enough to fall down.

"Once you have some dance skills, your first dance with somebody is really neat, you watch it—it's a ritual. The guy will turn the lady right, and turn her left and maybe do a little position change, and if she's continuing to stay with it, he'll continue to pass and do more complex things. It's almost like a first date. It's kind of a drama: you see what she's interested in, how far she wants to go and in what direction. When there's a little resistance or lack of interest—or inability—you kind of move away and see where the boundaries are. Then you work within those boundaries. And that first dance, with two people who dance well, is exquisite to dance and just fabulous to watch, because you can see that working together going on!"

"Well, I'm thinking of calling this book *Two by Two*, kind of romantic," I say.

"One other thing about two-step, for this interview. It's one dance, unlike basketball, where people learn the fundamentals *last*."

(Obviously this is a big complaint with him, trying as he is to teach fundamentals.)

"Yes," I agree, though I too was that way. I started the worst dance, tango, first and wound up last at two-step, and even in two-step I wanted to move straight to all the turns, rather than learn how to move right.

"First you learn footwork, second you learn moves. But all people care about are 'moves.' And then they get this real tortured choreography where they're out of position and off bal-

ance, and feet are flying, and then, finally, to smooth it out—
then they learn fundamentals—you know, how to turn."

"Yes." (At the time I didn't know how right he was, so I
skipped over this part.) "But at least in two-step, you can kind of
do an okay pass and nobody cares, and at least you don't have to
wear high heels!"

"Yeah, good point. But you do need to wear cowboy boots—
which are restrictive. And so are the cowboy hats. But because
of the kind of restrictions they put on you, it makes a slick style.

"I don't do privates so much anymore. I don't have as much
time and I don't need the money quite as much, but when I do,
they want to know. 'Tell us what we ought to do.' So we start
working on fundamentals, because they have plenty of material,
they just weren't educated well. So we work on fundamentals
for ten or fifteen minutes, this is in privates, and you can see
them start to get impatient, and you know what's coming, but
you kind of wait because it's like feeding someone vegetables
before they eat dessert.

"You wait a little while, then they say, 'We really appreciate
what you're doing, teaching us fundamentals, but we want
moves.' And you know it's coming so you get moves ready to go
and you know what they're doing, they're telling you that they
are intermediate-level dancers. Once they get more moves, then
they can dance, doing three or four numbers without repeating
anything. Then they need to clean it up."

"Right," I agree, though I'd be *happy* to be an intermediate-
level dancer.

"So, two by two," he says.

We pause. The main thing about the two-step that makes it
work, one of the fundamentals even more important than footwork, is posture. It's something I found difficult to remember to

do, but when I did remember it, and if I was dancing with a better dancer, they could do a lot more things with me, turnwise.

"Ever since I started doing two-step, every time I go tango dancing, they say 'You're too tight, you're too tight.' In tango, they want your upper body like liquid; and then *not*, but in a different way."

"That's interesting, how is your tango?"

"All my dancing has gotten a lot better, but in tango and salsa your upper body is very soft, almost limp. So in this, it's like the Viennese waltz for your back, but now my arm is so tired. I'd like to take one week, do all these different dances, and see if I could do it."

"What a challenge. One week, and just . . . That would be a great structure for a story in itself!"

"Hey, that's true. The basic thing is to be led, which is the hard thing—to wait. How long has your partner in the class been dancing?"

"Well, she's more used to freestyle, she's still working on her frame."

"She is?" It seemed to me his partner was the last word in everything; she even wore a hat sometimes.

"If you're talking about the structure of the two-step, the frame is like that; the frame keeps functioning as a unit. But that's what you need. If you don't have that, if you're too loosey-goosey, then it turns into a wrestling match—just a tangle of moves."

"Sometimes in a dance, if you just try to do this one thing, then everything else falls into place, it's the frame in two-step."

"You know what's fun to do is to sit someplace and pick a couple who did not come together, and just watch them for the whole dance. See what kind of a story their dancing tells. Is this a hotdogger trying to show off? Does he lack confidence; how does that affect the dance? If you're afraid of a dog, the dog has no respect for you—and if your lead lacks confidence, your partner has no respect for you. You see all kinds of things being acted out.

"Is he sensitive to his partner, is he looking at her? Is she looking at him? Is there any kind of partnership, does it look like a hookup deal?"

"It's hard," I add, "if the girl can't follow. One man I knew dancing with this friend of mine—she couldn't follow so he followed her. The next day she called me up and said, 'I really like your friend; he really knows how to lead.'"

"You described a good Texas Two-stepper perfectly. You've got to adapt to your partner, you do something and have no clue what's going on, you take it and turn it into something—traffic intervenes, you adapt."

"Plus you can see how people are under pressure too."

"And for someone who hasn't danced, you're out there in front of everybody. So when you start, anyway, you feel like everybody is just looking at you and nobody else. The fact of the matter is, nobody is looking at you, and if you're not very good, they're *especially* not looking at you."

"Well, I guess I can't call it partner dancing, it's too . . ."

"In country and western, couples dancing is the two-step and waltz. Partner dancing is the choreographed dances like Cowboy Cha-cha or the Horseshoe."

"Well, it's a funny way to do the cha-cha, but it does look great."

"One thing about country dancing, it welcomes any kind of influence. You've got some ballroom, you've got some salsa—bring it aboard, and let's mix it in—it's like America! In France, they don't allow any words that aren't French because it's bad form, but America, it's like, bring it all. Of course, we have a language with half a million words, but it's made up of everything! Country dancing is like that—if you have another dance form, you're welcome, as long as it's adapted to the basic rules of line of dance."

"Whereas you go to ballroom and you try and form a dance lane around the floor, you're going to get booted!"

Paul says, "It used to be a thing, people danced in the general direction of line of dance, but now nobody knows this anymore. So they crash into each other. In the old days, they used to have line of dance. But now, women are afraid to dance with guys, because they're afraid they aren't good enough."

"I always think if a man's a really good dancer, then he can lead anything," I say.

"You're right, you adapt to your partner. If she gets confused, or if she dances forward rather than backward, then she dances backward. You can find that out real easily. The irony is it's kind of a dilemma: country wants to be accepted for being real polite. And it is the politest dance form. Women can come in by themselves and feel comfortable and they're not going to get hit on, there aren't problems like that, or they're very rare. Whereas you go to a rock-and-roll place . . . But another part of the appeal of country is its raunchy hard-drinking roots, so you want to keep that, because that gives it a little bit of edge. You don't want to get it cleaned up too much!"

"You're right, that's for people who like to stay up past nine o'clock at night!" I know because I'm the worst person for going home early, complaining I've had enough.

One of the great things about dancing, we both agreed, is "There's something that's revealed about the way you dance and dress and present yourself, how sunny, or open, or not."

After talking so much about his teaching Paul admitted that if he had the time and money, he'd probably want to learn a particular dance himself—West Coast Swing, from Phil Adams.

"Phil Adams hasn't competed and won championships and that sort of thing, but he runs a studio operation, he's a nice guy, he has good material, he just attracts good dancers and people get along. So there's a whole swing community that is under his flag.

"My dream is to take lessons from Phil for a couple of nights a week, for a couple of years. The only thing that would keep me from doing West Coast all the time is that I love two-step too much. And the only thing that keeps me from doing those two all the time is, I love Pony Swing too much."

"Well, I love the waltz too much," I said.

"It's nice to be pulled by things that you love, rather than repelled by things you hate. A lot of these things have a lifetime of two or three or four years where you go through this passionate intensity . . ."

"A love affair with a dance."

"It's nice to have something like that, to give a focus to your life."

"It's much better than staying home and watching television," I agree, although I have a great capacity for that, too.

"Think of the exercise. From just the two-step you walk four miles an hour; you dance for two hours, you've walked eight miles plus upper body movement. Now, if you told somebody you just walked eight miles, they would think that you were a fitness freak!"

"But people are afraid; they hate their bodies so much, they can't even get themselves there, and they'd look so much better after they've been doing it for two months."

"You really have a way," Paul said, "of hitting the nail on the head. Let's imagine that an active two-step is like going down Niagara Falls in a barrel. Now, Pony Swing would be like riding the tea cups in an amusement park. Constantly spinning and going around in circles."

"Is Pony Swing like West Coast, only faster and crazier?"

"It's like Cajun, except you dance just within the width of your shoulders and you're always turning, you never land in the same place twice."

"Who developed this dance?"

"It's a Cajun dance; in the Southeast they drop on the two and four beats of the measure—in the Southwest they drop on the one and three of each measure. Next time I see you, have a DJ play a Pony and I'll show you enough of it to get the feel of it!

"With a good Pony partner, you'll clear the floor. Clapping and cheering . . . and another thing you find at the workshops, it used to be that the women outnumbered the men two to one, and now it's the men outnumbering the women. Women are always coming and saying they can't find a good guy with a good job who's wholesome and sociable. But these guys are out there, walking out on the floor, which takes immense courage, and there's no partner for them, so they have to go back and sit down. You know that they're hurt, but the guys have discovered that if they can dance, they've got a social life that, you know, Elvis would take his hat off to."

Paul was raised in San Diego, the home of Tony Bill and Anita Loos, a great town for unbelievable people.

He has two daughters; one is an architect, the other is a flight attendant and works for Delta Airlines. His son just graduated from Moody Bible Institute in Chicago. "He's real devout," Paul says, somewhat amazed. "He would come to some of the dances and laugh and laugh at me. Now he's up in Seattle waiting to get into the police academy; eventually he wants to be an FBI agent. He's a great kid, he's funny as can be," he says.

We chatted into the night, I wishing I were a different kind of person, who could wind up with a man like this, taking Phil Adams's West Coast Swing class on into the next millennium. If only I were a Republican and not the daughter of a Trotskyist . . . But alas.

Another thing about the two-step is that it's the only dance not overrun with Jews (like tango, salsa, ballroom, or even swing). Though I'm only half Jewish and at the time looked like Betty Grable's sister because my hair was so platinum, I don't think I could live in a dance that was so cheerful and unneurotic. Even though I complain neurotically about how morbidly critical and mean the other dancers are, how could I stand a life of all Mockingbird Hill chirpiness?

The truth of the matter is, I like to be the only cheerful one in a roomful of people in high dudgeon. I *enjoy* driving my genius friends crazy with my dumb act, pretending I don't know what they're talking about when they get obstreperous (which makes them worse). I enjoy being the Mockingbird Hill spokeswoman, in a town where lately the riots, floods, fires, maniacs, and, worst of all, traffic have made being cheerful a high-wire act.

The truth is that as much as I love doing the two-step, as well as I've finally learned to hold my frame and thus be led by better dancers to look like one of those Valkyrie Ice Skaters myself sometimes, and as much as I even love the line dances like the Rocket and the Toosh Push, I'm just too Russian a Jew, too imbued with Cossack genetic memories, too recently arrived by steerage boat to Ellis Island. I have too Yiddish a grandfather and too much respect for what my family believed was culture to marry a man in a white cowboy hat and fade into a western sunset.

What's really the oddest, though, is that my mother was raised in Texas yet all her adult life regarded anything country as beyond the pale, as too hokey and low-class for words. Now in her old age and with dementia, she is cheered up only by the Nashville station, and *really* likes best the guys in hats, or the dancers. In fact, sometimes on our forty-eight cable stations, the Nashville one is the *only* thing she can enjoy. The only thing she can see.

My mother was a girl from a very small town, Sour Lake, Texas, who came to the big city and married millennia of tragedy, culture, and survival in the form of a Jewish boy with shiny black hair, the first violinist of the Los Angeles Philharmonic, a far, far cry from cowboy hats. But would I be happy the rest of my life in the conventions and restrictions of country two-step, the boots (well, I am not going *anywhere* without my Evenin' Stars, but still), the hats, the denim, the line of dance, the sad American voices singing real songs with real lyrics? The whole scene has a lot to recommend it—and I have friends in Nashville, an in with the Judds—maybe I should just become a country girl myself.

I mean, at least they never caved in to rock and roll, no matter how much money people involved were rolling in. There are older stars, there are older women stars, they *stay* stars—Emmylou Harris has gray hair. If she'd been rock 'n' roll, she'd probably be dead like poor Graham Parsons. And in country dancing, if you can get up and do it you're not too old, that's the only rule.

Oh, well. It's something to ponder.

In the meantime I did take Paul McClure to see Orlando Paiva the tango master when he came back to Los Angeles and gave workshops. I took him to my wonderful friend Kassie's house in that beautiful part of Hancock Park where she lives, and I had forgotten that to outsiders Hancock Park looks like vast wealth personified, like Southampton to Gatsby.

All the great dancers were at Kassie's that night: Enio from Let's Dance L.A., Renée Victor, Maurice, the wonderful Doz, and Loreen Arbus, who has a tango troupe now of her own, but not Orlando because, of course, he's always the last to get anywhere.

When he finally arrived, with Michael Espinoza and Yolanda, a *thrill* ran through everyone there. Orlando was dressed better than anyone on earth, his shoes looked better polished, his jacket of finer fabric, he just *glowed.*

Then, of course, they couldn't find the CD selection they wanted, which was really a theatrical stall because they had a live tango trio arriving, and they did arrive, finally, after nine false starts on the tango CD.

So there we were, Paul and I, and the live tango band began. Orlando and Yolanda began to do this tango that just *riveted* the house to attention; we were drooling, it was simply too much. Every pause, every move, folded, inverted, controlled—it was devastation in romance.

The whole room shimmered; there was nothing on earth like it.

Afterward, as Paul and I drove away, he said, "It's like I'm still in afterglow."

You know, I don't think I could give up this much art for even true happiness and only the two-step.

I know the phrase "Would you rather be right or happy" is used to make people see the light and their stupidity, but if you change that to "Would you rather have art or be happy?"—well, I don't see how anyone could be happy *without* art.

Of course, this is the dilemma of my life and not really your problem; however, please send me a fax or postcard if you've got a solution for me. At any rate, if country was good enough for Ray Charles, Willie Nelson, and Patsy Cline, it's got to be good enough for me, and no matter how snobby people are about the music, it's American and it never went rock and roll, it never succumbed to *that* mediocrity. So maybe the dancing is great, too.

The Two Sides of Tango

Part One: Gigolo, the Silly Side of Tango

Most people take up tango because none of the other dances are complicated or wild enough for them anymore; they need a challenge.

Me, I began doing it after two months of ballroom dancing at the Hollywood YMCA. Not because I'd mastered the waltz, or rumba, or cha-cha, or fox-trot and needed a challenge, but because I saw the show *Tango Argentino*. Then there was Orlando Paiva, who was teaching right here in L.A.—beginners, $5 per class. It seemed so cheap—little did I know.

The tango scene in Los Angeles is ambivalent, and I don't know how I feel about it myself. On the one hand, it's the most beautiful dance, but then, as a friend of mine overheard recently, "a little tango goes a long way."

For me, doing it at certain times with certain people, like Michael Walker, who used to teach at the Studio for Performing Arts, was extremely exciting, like flying over an old European city with vampires like Lestat and some victim, meeting only other equally depraved vampires along the way. A dance so exciting and so fast, you don't even know how you got that way, but you're flying. With Michael Walker, it was a dance of reckless impatience; only an aristocrat would know it and be unafraid to do this dance of death in a baroque city filled with modern passions. And a few times when I danced with various great men, I have felt that maybe this wasn't such a terrible dance after all, it was so thrilling.

On the other hand, it seems to be a dance that, in Los Angeles anyway, draws fewer and fewer devotees. In San Francisco, apparently, they've got a tango scene together, complete with newspaper. In New York, too, they claim to have a bunch of people crazy for tango. In Buenos Aires, on the other hand, I've heard people say tango is no longer what it was. The only place in the world you can go outside at night and be sure to find clubs with tango music and dancers is Santiago, Chile.

In Los Angeles, all scenes are bushwhacked and peremptorily ignored by others—once friends, now enemies. If someone starts any event in tango on a Tuesday, someone will open a competing event just on that day, as though there were nine million tango maniacs in L.A. rather than forty-seven.

"In tango, there are eight students, twelve teachers, and a hundred critics," a friend of mine who was involved told me. He, too, is puzzled by the conflicting impulses that tear everything down every time someone tries to build anything up.

"I want to 'invite' you to this milonga we're having," people call to say. "It's ten dollars, but that includes . . ."

I myself, uncertain I even like tango anyway, have kept away from knowing how downhill it's been going by running off to two-step places. At least there after a certain amount of practice you get reasonably proficient, and they don't expect you to leak money, as they do in tango. They want money for lessons, money for "honoring" this one, money for clubs, and minimums. And one can go to these places and spend money, but the chance of actually *dancing* much or even once, well . . . In all other dances, you get to dance all the time and people who dance with you will actually buy you diet Cokes, not expect you to pay for them like a gigolo.

"In Buenos Aires," a woman told me, "if you go to a tango bar and dance with one of those guys more than twice and don't pay them, they *pout*."

In Los Angeles the problem with tango is always money—or people dancing so well they won't dance with you. Or dancing so badly, *you* won't dance with *them*.

When I first started, in 1987 or so, everybody complained about going to Norah's, this cozy and pretty little Bolivian nightclub in North Hollywood with food so laced with lard that people soon learned never to eat even the rolls, they were too good to be true. Every weekend there they had two bands, tango and salsa, and on Saturday night people interested in tango would go. Maybe they'd even see Orlando Paiva dance with one of his students, or at least his students, who, since I was one of them, yearned and pined to dance and complained there were never enough men.

But then, tango is a dance of complaints, and it was all anybody did, complain about Norah's, about not enough of the right dance partners. Yet every single Saturday night, there everyone was—for years. A tango paradox.

Finally, Orlando Paiva, who was our great inspiration, returned to Argentina. Of course, it was better for his health that he left because at Norah's all he ate were those steaks covered with eggs and tons of french fries, which is not good for a person who got out of breath from walking one block.

We were all sad that he had gone; everyone owed all his or her tango ability to him. Yet factions built up because some still tried to do his kind of tango (which is basically impossible unless you have the balance of a stork and the bravado of Michael Walker), but some just wanted to have fun.

The scene in Los Angeles fell apart, although people still went to Norah's, and still did tango. The only person remotely in charge was a very nice and stylish dancer named Felix Chavez, who got a group of four couples together to do "shows" at Norah's or Pasión, another club that opened in Studio City. Pasión was everything everyone complaining about Norah's wanted, except Pasión opened with tango on a paradoxical night, Tuesday.

Kassie (and even I) and several people had tried to get tango started at the Atlas on Tuesday nights. But when Pasión opened, it too decided Tuesday was tango night and destroyed the Atlas possibility, breaking our hearts on this side of town for some mean-spirited tango reason none of us could comprehend. I mean, Pasión had just opened, it could have tango night on any night, yet it opened on Tuesday, stamping out Atlas's attempt. Why? No one knew.

The guy who was willing to oversee tango at the Atlas, Mark, then found a place in downtown L.A. called Valentino's, which people hardly complained about at all, and there was a scene there on Mondays. But Valentino's had to change its name because there was a great Italian restaurant in Santa Monica named that. Eventually we called it "the Hideaway," but this, too, recently closed and now everyone's sad. Of course, everyone in tango wants a beautiful nightclub like Valentino's where there's tons of free parking, you don't fear for your life, and the place is mysterious yet cozy. But that place closed, because dancers cannot keep places open, only diners can.

In the meantime, since Orlando left, a gorgeous professional dance troupe made up of Loreen Arbus, one of Orlando's students, and her partner, Alberto, has formed. It is supposed to be wonderful and they teach, but they don't, as far as I know, go out dancing anywhere in public, because if they found a place we'd all hear about it, clamor in tango droves, and soon it would be closed from lack of funds.

Michael Espinoza and his partner, the beautiful Yolanda Rossi, both gorgeous dancers, have a "tango bar" right off Hollywood Boulevard. Maurice tells me he likes to go "practice" there because there are usually never enough people to dance with, so there's plenty of room to dance and nobody will step on his feet, like at Norah's or El Floridita for salsa. I have been there, and because it's on Cahuenga Boulevard off Hollywood Boulevard, the neighborhood is too intense for most people—Hollywood having such a bad rep nowadays from all the dope fiends. But now they're moving to a new place in Westwood—L.A. Dance Experience—which might be a better place for it all. Except of course they're having it on the wrong night, Friday.

Sometimes I wonder if tango makes people contentious and impossible, or if people who are that way are drawn to tango. They use their power in the dance to drive the tango world into splintered factions.

In any other dance scene, if people knew one group were starting up on a certain day, they'd go there and use another day for their thing, thus enriching the whole scene, not trying to hack days off for themselves.

And worst of all, of course, the men who dance well and get involved in setting up these dance things, they never want to dance again—tango becomes a burden rather than a joy. The whole way this dance is, even if I could dance well and could wear high heels and did have a right foot I could balance on without shattering pain, I would take off for other things, country dancing or Cajun especially.

While the city of Los Angeles falls apart in earthquakes, fires, floods, crazy racial unrest, and scandals like O.J. and Nicole, we in the cultural community and the spirit of art are just as much a scandal. Tearing apart other people's scenes, making it impossible for tango to survive, sticking impossible roadblocks in the way of every attempt to keep alive a dance that, in some weird way, keeps those who love it alive too. It's a paradox is what it is.

When I first began doing tango, if I had studied with Felix Chavez for six months, I would at least have learned the basics—been able to follow and at least feel like I was dancing. My friend Jim Hines told me in so many words how much fun he had at Pasadena Ballroom Dance, just learning to do so-so ballroom with people on an equally so-so footing. But I didn't listen to what was probably advice, I just kept hoping to evolve into something marvelous like Orlando, when in fact I was unable to so much as follow because I was a nervous wreck.

I was ambivalent about doing tango too because I saw how all the other women could move in high heels, and I knew I never would.

High heels just killed my previously fractured foot, and my will to dance was unequal to the idea of ignoring pain like Gelsey Kirkland. Those dancers with bleeding toes, who do it anyway, was a level I could only dream about. In tango the women have to have feet like steel and bounce like rubber all in elegant high heels, even though, too, other dancers with spike heels are likely to stab their feet and worsen any condition—which happens all the time.

In tango there is a moment before the dance begins where the man very lightly touches the woman and she is so adept, she sort of can be knocked over with a feather as he touches her. This was a feeling I never had; I couldn't be knocked over at all; I was just so unequal to any basic move.

Now that I have some ballroom dance experience and know the kind of squishy condition the woman has to be in to be led, I can sometimes, if I'm really sure of my partner, do tango not too badly, though I now prefer milongas. At least with those you feel elated afterward. That floating fox-trot feeling abounds. Milonga, which in Spanish means "dance," is also the name in Argentina of this hilariously fun kind of march-beat dance that is so fast, it's just adorable. All women wish they were doing it all the time, as do men because, as one told me, "It's not so serious."

Me, I am glad I went to all these other dance experiences to write this book, because it's nice to find places where I feel I belong, where I never feel I am a total washout. This is a feeling one gets sitting there not dancing tangos, in a scene where there's not enough men, and the men there no longer want to dance anyway.

There are plenty of amazingly beautiful women tango dancers in our scene, Kassie being one of the best. She's been dancing tango for ten years now; high heels are her métier (she never heard of Reeboks until last summer when she sprained her foot). Yet she claims to prefer cha-chas and West Coast, or the Hustle, which is a dance now coming back because everybody is into everything again. Every dance she does, she puts herself so totally into it that she's great fun to watch. And in Los Angeles, she's an inspiration to a lot of women who wish they could get dressed up, go out, and look like her—they follow her into the ladies' room and beg her, "How do you do it?"

"Do what?" she asks, actually wondering.

Her secrets for the "world of men" are easy. When she enters any dance situation, she carefully greets every man she knows there, saying, "I do hope we get a dance together, but you know, I'm leaving at ten-thirty, so if we don't dance by then . . ."

This is how she gets all the men to ask her to dance right away, and since she does leave most places by 10:30 (before they start to get drunk and no fun), she usually dances all the first dances with the best men.

It would seem to me that since a woman arrives at a dance place all dressed up and dying to dance, men would *know* she wants to dance with them, and it should go unspoken: this is the deal. But Kassie realized long ago in her Hustle days that every single time she had to explain she wanted to dance with them, and always included she was leaving early so she could dance with them *soon* rather than one in the morning or something. Men, even ones who want to dance, will get to a place, sit down, and claim they're not in the mood dance after dance, being the balkers they are when it comes to women.

The salsa scene was so grisly that I would see perfectly gorgeous women arrive with friends, all dressed to kill, and nobody would ask them to dance *ever*, because they didn't know them and didn't know whether they could dance or not. If they saw one of these women dancing with someone eventually, and saw they could dance, then they'd ask them. But no men want to be first—except Maurice, who always finds undanced-with women, dances with them, and suddenly everyone's dancing with them.

"I just give them a few twirls," he says, "and they're off!"

But even Maurice could get into a "Who likes dancing anyway?" mood if he thinks people expect him to do something he's not in the mood for. Of course, Maurice has been involved with tango since it came to town but he hates Norah's, and hates most of the places tango goes on, and yet if you saw him dance—even with me—you'd think it was the passion of his life.

I have always had a love-hate relationship with tango. Love brought about by getting all dressed up in outrageously sexy clothes, doing high drama on the dance floor, and having Orlando Paiva as an inspirational figure, an impossibly beautiful dancer who fills the very air of tawdry and smoldering L.A. with aspirations beyond anyone's wildest dreams. And hate because I cannot balance on the ball of my right foot—even in ballet slippers, even in Evenin' Stars, much less in high heels—which in tango is the very dance itself.

I hated tango because the people it drew to it were the very most crazed and critical monsters of all the world finding something to fight about in every damned thing. I hated it because after spending so much time, money, amazement, and love, all I wound up with was the ball of my right foot being unable to do so much as a "boleo," much less those incredible "ochos," which demand so much balance and fire.

I loved tango because often, when I was really doing it a lot, I got the feeling that if I hung on, I'd be flying over decadent cities of times past, cities of exiles weird enough to invent this dance. Cities where Carlos Gardel sang day and night about lost tango love, and where girls washed up on shore as green mermaids, the sea all in their hair. Cities where those who did tango slashed the soles of their shoes crosswise with razor blades so they could move more smoothly. Cities of endless bordellos, where the dance of the gauchos and the dance of the whores melted into the "Porteño," the dance of the port of Buenos Aires. Beautiful air, beautiful night, beautiful dancers—the vampires of long ago, when those who could flew over the world, bringing memories of past love, memories of dancers past, memories of the world before Louis Armstrong came along and the dancers all turned to swing.

In one of the ballroom dancing magazines, a champion West Coast Swing dancer remarked that she never went anywhere people did West Coast when she danced, because she was too besieged by people trying to be taught what she was doing. She said she could only go to country places, two-step ones, "because there," she said, "I was just a dancer among dancers."

It's amazing to read that, because with tango, those like

Kassie, who wants to be a dancer among dancers, would, if she weren't so philosophical, feel betrayed by those other dancers.

I don't like to say too much about tango, because like everyone else, everything I say sounds bitter, contentious, critical, and, perhaps, a bit like love. It's just the worst dance you could ever do, I don't know why anyone likes it, and one of these days, I'm going to never do it again.

Just not yet, okay. Just one last tango, here in L.A., before I die.

Just one, or at least a milonga.

Part Two: The Serious Side of Tango

Orlando Paiva was gone for eight years when all we did was wish he'd come back. Finally, Michael Espinoza and Yolanda Rossi went down to Santiago, Chile, in 1995 and persuaded Orlando to come to Los Angeles (well, Glendale) and stay with them in their home. I went to visit him during his first visit back to Los Angeles.

I parked on a nice street with lots of trees and lawns. Orlando was nervous, because he didn't know whether or not I was going to take a picture, and if he was to be photographed, he was going to get into this unbelievably sharp outfit he could never dream of wearing. Michael and Yolanda helped translate for me.

"When he expressed an interest in coming to Los Angeles, when we were in Chile, we said sure, that would be great because everyone would love to see him again, and he was interested in us 'handling' everything for him here, taking care of all the details. I couldn't believe it!"

Michael laughed; it was as if he had caught the magic carpet and the magic carpet had *offered* to let him ride.

"Of course there were people in Santiago like Doz, but Orlando already knew me; I talked to him about Yolanda . . ."

"To be fair, Doz was the one who made us see it was important, to go to Chile no matter what and see Orlando."

"So from that time until now, we were raising everything for Orlando."

"And you just stay here," I asked Orlando. "You haven't gotten into any fistfights or anything?"

"No," he replied, laughing at my joke, but then he always laughed at my jokes even back in the old days.

"He's always happy," Yolanda told me, "he never complains. He adapts very well."

"When he wakes up in the morning, the first thing he looks for is something to laugh at. He starts the day off like that and continues the whole day that way. We've been very fortunate; while Orlando is staying here the reception has been overwhelming. Interestingly enough, when we went to San Francisco the same thing happened there. He was legendary there as well, and everyone wanted to know Orlando Paiva, and as in Los Angeles nobody wanted him to leave. He also has a following in Santiago, but fortunately, Yolanda had already trained enough in his style, so that Orlando asked her to dance with him while he was here."

It was the first time they danced together in Los Angeles, at Kassie's party, where I had taken Paul McClure the two-step teacher with me. We saw Orlando and Yolanda dancing and it was so breathtaking. . . .

They told me Orlando was coming back that July (which he did) and going back to San Francisco, which he did also, and I said, "You should have a tango boat that goes up and down the coast—the SS *Tango*."

"Sure, it's a great idea," Yolanda agreed. "That's one thing Orlando wanted to do, take his teaching to other parts of the world. He's making a teaching video, with his explanation—a series of teaching videos, his opinions of tangos, his own way to teach."

Orlando, meanwhile, has been sitting here; he says nothing, just laughs.

"Another good thing about Orlando here in Los Angeles is that since he's been here, there are about five more milongas here."

"It seems to me that more ordinary people are coming to tango, not just dancers."

"I agree that many more people are coming to tango, even ballet dancers."

"I believe that people understand that dancing together is much more interesting and nicer than dancing apart. It is more a human, physical thing."

"Do you teach in Rosario?" Rosario is a three-hour drive from Buenos Aires; it's a beautiful city.

"Yes, I teach in Rosario, it's not as many students as I should have but there are young people, that's the most important thing. Really young couples are coming to tango. Eighteen to thirty years."

"How long have you been teaching?"

"Forty years."

"How long you have you been dancing?"

"Fifty years, since I was a child, since I can remember."

"And it's always tango, the milonga, and the waltz?"

"No, no, no, everything, a long time ago I teach social dancing in Argentina."

"He used to teach all other dances," Yolanda said, "before he taught tango. He used to be sure they could dance to all other music before they learn tango."

(See, nobody told me this; I would have gone and learned ballroom first then.)

"So then you came to America and you were a machinist, what a waste."

"Yes, I always teach besides working, I find a way to teach on the side, all the time, so that's why I don't consider it a waste of my time."

"Do you like other kinds of dancing, the ballet?"

"No."

"What do you like?"

"I enjoy more the social dancing, good music and good singers, I like to be close to the performers. Things on the stage far away, no."

It turned out he had seen a little of the two-step dancers and found it very enjoyable. I also learned from Sonny Watson that they'd taught classes in the same bar, so he must know about West Coast Swing too.

"Orlando teaches in Chile four months of the year," Yolanda said. "When I saw how he teaches there, how he is respected and how people love him over there, I said to myself, we need Orlando in Los Angeles."

"When he is here it's great, but when he goes away . . ."

"Something happens different," Yolanda finished, remarking on his magic and charisma. "When he comes it's a passion, people want to follow him.

"He also wants it included, he thinks it's very important, that people dance tango as a *social* dance, dance together enjoying themselves, not like they're on the stage or performers. He wants to let people know, he thinks it's very important, that it's a social dance.

"He wants the couple to be together and understand the dance and dance to the music. Steps are nice, but they're not that important."

Orlando, knowing that this is going to be in a book and important, decides to pull himself together for a quote for the public. "He says that people dancing tango should learn the correct way to move the feet because that makes tango more elegant, and it is important to be really *into* the music, to really know the music, in order to dance to the music. He says people should learn to move around the dancing floor with a lot of respect for the other dancers. It's very, very important, because if you don't respect the other couples then you lose your concentration and everybody else on the floor is the same way. But if you move the right way then everybody else enjoys it too."

"There is no age for tango," Orlando adds. "Anybody from a child to an older person, it doesn't matter what age you are, you can dance tango. Tango does a lot of good things for you, because it motivates you emotionally and physically. So if you start dancing tango you will be incredible physically, and motivated to have health, to go out, to have friends—tango is a very incredible link to a lot of things."

"It certainly did get me moving," I agree.

"Couples, they raise their children and they are retired. When they start dancing tango, the passion between them revives again, they start like a second life again. It is so important, it is compared to adopting a child, because now they have a new motivation for living, something that really gets into them and makes them enjoy the last years of their lives with more passion."

"That's a great way to put it. If you adopt a child it motivates you to do a lot of things; tango is the same way. It motivates you to get dressed, to meet people, everything that you do with tango."

"People don't dance and they think they can't dance because it's been too long."

Later we discussed *Tango Argentino* and how it changed the world.

I said, "A lot of people in the world used to dance tango, but not the Argentine tango. They used to dance the tango that they imagined was danced, but when the whole world saw the beauty of the Argentine tango on the stage, that's when the whole world got interested in that company. Because they saw the difference between what they used to do and what Argentine tango was. For instance, here they advertised the company at least one year before they came to Los Angeles. They used to advertise pieces of the different couples in the show on television, and from only the advertisement even before they saw the show they created, people were already, "Ahhh, for tango . . .""

"Then when the people from America got interested just from the advertisement, imagine what they felt after the seeing the show—because many people saw the show many times. I started to have more students immediately after that."

"So an interest from the show came from the television advertisement, and people started wanting to take tango."

"I used to teach before that, but to the Argentines, to Raúl in nineteen seventy-eight at the Argentine Society, in an Argentine club on eighth and Alvarado. Since I came to America in nineteen seventy."

Yolanda jumped in. "The interest in tango here in Los Angeles with Orlando—there were probably ten people interested in tango here in L.A., maybe the whole United States, we don't know. But when *Tango Argentino* came and he started teaching, from there it started to build and flourish to what it is now. He also did the same thing in San Francisco. He is also the first tango teacher to go to Japan. So in all of his life, this is what he wanted to do and it was a dream come true."

"In Argentina it wasn't being danced much either."

"But when he came here, tango came with him," Yolanda added. "The other great thing is he started so many couples, Michael Walker and Loren, Loreen Arbus and Alberto, us—we are together, Michael and me, because of Orlando. His style was so strong, we were here learning his from his tapes.

"That's the beauty of a good teacher, he inspires so many different people, and he finds a way for a student to learn the way he teaches."

I left the happy home of Yolanda, Michael, and Orlando as their honored guest, and it is amazing that after he's been gone only a few months, Los Angeles has fallen back into its old paradoxical ways.

One woman in San Francisco, where he had gone and given a seminar, told me, "He just placed my foot in the right spot and suddenly the whole dance went up a quantum leap."

This woman believes, however, that though Orlando's style is spectacular it isn't for everyone. She says it is only for himself, for the way he's built and how he moves naturally. She thinks that as great as he is, tango should be for everyone. She can afford to be philosophical, though, because she's married to her own private tango teacher-partner and doesn't have to worry about being asked to dance.

Still, I am ambivalent about tango, if not about Orlando, who is such an inspiration. He is only doing his job, trying to teach people the way he moves because that's all people want out of life when they see him—to learn to be him.

Me, I don't know, now that I'm wearing my hair up in a pony-tail, and have got the Cajun "look" so down I can do it with one hand tied behind my back; now that all my Michael Morrison earrings from tango at the Atlas are sort of gathering dust; and now that my gorgeous famous Hanna Hartnell skirt of irides-cent silk taffeta died in Hong Kong . . .

Maybe if I didn't have to wear high heels, if they let you do tango in Evenin' Star Boots . . .

4

Cajun Dancing and the Fais-Dodo:
Laissez les bons temps rouler

People who do West Coast Swing think it's so great that all other dances would *be* West Coast Swing, if only people *knew.* They are the ultimate dance police and blame "country dancers" for bringing down the quality of the dancing. Whereas, in fact, if it weren't for, say, the Cajun dances twice a month a lot of people wouldn't even want to do a waltz.

In the movie *The Big Easy,* it looks as though New Orleans was just the nicest and most fun (except for the crime) place you'd ever get to go. A place where the Cajun police chief, when he dances with our Brooklyn heroine, is charm personified, and that indeed all Cajuns must be just as charming. That we ought to go right down there and just, well, "laissez les bons temps rouler."

The movie made it seem like even the regular police were not going to get too upset about anything not exactly right you did. So if you do this jitterbug and it looks kind of funny, well, there's no dance police there in Cajun things either.

Especially at a fais-dodo—that's the name of a Cajun place where dances go on. Fais-dodo is Cajun French baby talk for "put to sleep," as in putting the children to sleep so the adults can dance, dance, dance. Which goes to show those Cajuns didn't let grass grow under their feet just because they were married and had children—they *danced!* Couple dancing too, and they'd have these dances once a week in the town hall or someone's living room along with gumbo. A fais-dodo is as far away as you can get from the Dance Police: the music, the night, the gumbo, and you, *cher.*

Of all the dancing things they have in southern California right now, the Cajun dances at the War Memorial Hall in South Pasadena are, to me, the *most* of what you might mean by going to a dance. The most lyrical, the most seductive; in spirit the place is surrounded with magnolias and jasmine, it's just so *avec plaisir, cher!*

Even from afar, walking up the street, seeing the rather nice sized hall filled with live music, smelling of gumbo and people dancing, with a live band playing waltzes, the place seems festive and welcoming, as though at last the right combination of place and dance had come together. Whereas most dance places usually act like they're not really dance places, the floor's too small, the floor's cement, the neighborhood's dangerous, there's no parking, or else it costs too much to get in—like some $60 dinner or something. But then, I'm partial to visuals, being once a designer, and of course, being half Cajun myself, I am partial to these wild bands and the night and this particularly crazy music. It's all just hot sauce to me, and I was raised on Tabasco and gumbo by my mother at a time in America when onions and garlic were considered a shock.

"You'll have to marry an Italian," my mother said, "you like garlic so much." Of course, if you're going to do partner dancing, *everybody*'s got to eat that gumbo, so nobody will mind—at this fais-dodo, everyone does anyway because it's only $5. (Although next time I'll bring my own Tabasco; their hot sauce isn't hot enough for me.)

People dance so much, they get wringing wet and forget things like diets. It's always the right time for gumbo or jambalaya, or even a praline, a thing you can't get in New York (according to my cousin, who thinks if she opened a praline business, it might be the next big bad Seduction). In New York until they have a thing for themselves, like a Thai restaurant, they don't think they'd like it, but to me pralines are ooh-la-la. In New York, they have show tunes and it could help one forget they don't have pralines, but still . . . even New York could stand a fais-dodo, putting the children to bed, going out to do the Cajun jitterbug to a great Cajun band, dancing the night away, *cher.*

The great thing about the Cajun dance I recently went to, with the live band and the great floor and space, is that I could dance with practically anyone, which, in my opinion, is the way a dance should happen. There are even children there, the small children of Karen Hysell and Chuck, her husband, the ones who run this scene so brilliantly.

I even got to dance with this black man, six feet four inches tall, who took my hand with such elegance and grace, I felt like the Princess in Sleeping Beauty, except he was the Beast transformed. Every step he led me in, in both the jitterbug and the waltz, was something I (or anyone) could follow. But then, most of the men there, they know how to take a dance partner's hand. That's one thing about a Cajun or would-be Cajun, *cher,* they *know.*

Of course, there was one problematic dance partner. A man who looked both insane and misguided asked me to dance. A guy with too-blond hair, a too-tight shirt, shirt pocket loaded with what seemed like demented pamphlets, a man who took my hand like he had *no idea* at all, and who, as we danced, couldn't lead and didn't care. He was only waiting, in fact, for the dance to end so he could inflict on me a pamphlet from his pocket and say, "Have you given your heart to Jesus?"

"Ugh!" I said, backing away in horror, my half-Cajun genes aghast.

Imagine one of these Christians determined to convert people, going to a Cajun dance and looking for willing victims! Imagine a man so poor of spirit, he'd invade a place were people where so happy and so free, trying to instill the Christian Coalition freeze!

To me, the Cajuns have never been particularly maniacal religiously. As William Faulkner Rushton in his book *The Cajuns from Acadia to Louisiana* wrote, "Music of this sort is entirely too loose to be an effective vehicle for religious purposes, hero worship, or nationalism, which requires a martial orderliness of presentation Cajun music steadfastly denies. Cajun music is almost entirely secular and joyous. Cajun music tells us it is better to live a full life, even with its pitfalls, than simply to exist, and that a full life lies close at hand, sometimes even within oneself. Cajun music tells us it is better to sing loudly and laugh coarsely than to curse fate or grumble about the human condition. And Cajun music relentlessly tells us, over and over again, that it is better to love and to trust than to fight and to fear."

Then, of course, there was that other half of my genetic makeup, which came from my father, a Russian Jew born in Brooklyn—his parents fleeing the pograms, his family moving to Los Angeles in the twenties. My father's side of the family wouldn't be any too thrilled with "giving my heart to Jesus" either; in fact, they'd rise from their graves and smite me if I so much as considered such a feeble gesture. There are enough Holy Rollers in L.A.'s history without *me* joining "the flock."

Anyway, that poor guy dematerialized at the end of our dance, and I don't know if he went around asking every woman there his question, but let's hope secularism *rouler'*d right over him and left him for *mort*.

It was such a freakish moment, I almost forgot to write about it, but the contrast between the dance's deepest integrity and this poor stranger from an ugly mental state was enormous. It's hard to imagine a division wider than the one between how happy people were and how rottenly he alone danced. In every scene, of course, there are people who don't dance well, but to combine that with burning in hell if you don't buy their act, I mean, even Jesus wouldn't expect that of a convert. Not that Jesus seemed like much of a dancer himself; he was probably one of those guys who couldn't dance, so he had to make up this whole big "don't have fun or else" type religion to make his side look righteous—the Fun Police for people who can't dance.

Anyway, I had a lot of fun for two solid hours dancing my feet off, doing this Cajun jitterbug, which has all sorts of steps they don't use in East Coast Swing or anything else, all the while looking at people doing this jitterbug who were really great. I wonder if it's close to Pony Swing, the dance my *cher* Paul McClure did, winning world champion three times in Phoenix. It *looks* the same, but they're both so fast, you can't see them.

When it's a hot day at the War Memorial Hall the huge fans come on early, so people who regret the place doesn't have air-conditioning can feel the breeze. But one thing about dancers, no matter how cold it is they wind up sweating, and this evening, cool as it was for an August sunset, was as beautiful as could be. There was an orange-y sunset complete with a perfect orange sun. Unlike the moon, the sun when it sets is always completely round, whereas the moon, well, it's slivers, it's halves, it's quarters, it's full only once a month.

I got there around seven; the dance class begins at 7:30, which means at least fifteen minutes late there, if not more. So when I arrived, the musicians were setting up, the Acadiana Cajun Band, which people paid $10 at the door to hear. There were plenty of other $10 nights; the nights that were different were like when the D. L. Menard Cajun Band played and it cost $12—a "national treasure," they were billed.

It was so early, I thought I might be able to interview the teachers-stagers, Karen and Chuck Hysell. However, Chuck was doing sound checks, and when Karen arrived she was too preoccupied setting up and making sure her adorable small daughters didn't run around too much to do an interview.

"I can't talk now," she told me. "I can't even talk today, forget it, we'll do it some other time."

"Humph," I said. These Cajuns, they have principles—"don't bug me" being a mainstay.

I wandered around the hall and wound up talking to a woman who was in her early fifties. She told me her daughter in Denver turned her on to Cajun events, that she was so into the fais-dodos there. They had them twice a month there too and she even went to Lafayette for some kind of event.

"Last week I took my mother here," she said. "She's eighty-five. She didn't dance, but she was interested. She used to do contest dancing in Miami. Latin dancing years ago."

When Karen and her husband, both dressed in festive but not too dressy clothes, got up to teach the "free" dance, only about fifteen people had arrived. But somehow by the time the class began five minutes later, there were thirty people, guys who already knew how and were willing to help us who didn't.

Having taken this Cajun jitterbug class once before, I was able, this time, to do it more easily and even gracefully—which is something, considering they recommend acting as though you've been injured in one heel and have to favor the other foot, using only the ball of the foot you've injured. You'd think this would make for an extremely stupid-looking dance, but it turns out to look very graceful and sort of like an abandoned debutante limping out to dance.

Once I'd had the lesson I couldn't wait to go get me some jambalaya, which I poured half a cup of hot sauce on, but not hot enough to deter me from downing the whole thing easily. And once the band began to play and all these lovely men asked me to dance, I was so overjoyed I could finally do this dance, I didn't want to ever stop. Especially when they played the waltzes, which were so graceful and fun, you went practically the entire way around the floor, the men lead so fantastically.

At the Cajun dance, I met Bert Carlyle and he was such a wonderful dancer and so in love, currently, with Cajun dancing, that he agreed to be interviewed, even though, as I soon found out, Cajun dancing was not his only dance history. For me dancing with him was an uplifting experience, he was so *great*.

"I was dancing with my fiancée in the early eighties, disco, the Hustle, I loved that. We were into that, but she got ill and later died. So that was partly why I started taking ballroom at Pasadena City College in eighty-four and eighty-five, and then I went to Pasadena Ballroom Dance. It's a lot of fun. I stayed with them for at least a year and a half, and then I went to Let's Dance L.A. when Enion just started it. I was one of his first students, my partner and myself. I took everything with him."

"Pasadena Ballroom Dance is where people first come, and then they go to other places to hone their skills."

"Right, they find out what they want to do and then they learn the different areas they want to go into. We had a lot of people at the time into country western and we had another group into West Coast Swing. They went over to Sonny Watson. He's wonderful."

"What a dance," I say. "I cannot do it."

"West Coast in this area is the king of dances, and, as far as I'm concerned, of the swing dances. And then some of us went into more advanced ballroom, which Pasadena Ballroom Dance didn't have at that time. Then I went to Sloan and Sloan for more advanced classes; that basically is a ballroom place."

"Right." I remarked that I met a woman who was preparing to compete in Blackpool, England, the utmost strictly ballroom competition on earth today, as we know it. "I guess there, they prepare you for Blackpool."

"They're preparing you to compete, is what they're doing. I felt that's the finest instructor I ever had, her name was Sloan, she was just absolutely the finest."

"I don't want to do strictly ballroom, though," I insist, "because it's too . . ."

"I don't blame you, you get into that, you get into a different type of dancing. A competition dancer is not a social dancer. It's just not the same thing. The people you are with at Pasadena Ballroom Dance are social dancers, they dance for the fun of it."

"Right, that's what my book is about."

"I think you need to do that because that's an aspect of dancing that is not generally covered in the tapes or books that are currently available. The greatest dance for that, as you know, is Cajun. Because you don't have to know much to get Cajun, you just have to like the music. If you like the music, you'll do the dance. That's my theory anyway."

"Well, but people do a lot of moves."

"There's a little or there's a lot. If you watch, at a dance, people are just standing there, doing one thing all night long, and then there are other people who do all sorts of stuff. Then you get some people like Ernie who will be dipping the ladies and flipping the ladies. When you see this kind of thing on a dance floor it's wonderful because it's what I call cutting edge—it's right there. No dance studio will pick it up because they can't, it's moving too fast for them. It's not a dance, it's evolving."

"I am Cajun, that's the fortunate thing. So I can do this."

"Well, I'm not a bit Cajun and I still can do it."

We pause to think about things, then he adds, "When I went to Chuck's class, and I've been many times, one of the things he mentioned (and he's the only instructor I've ever seen whose done this) was, 'Don't worry about these instructions, just go out and have fun and learn to do it and put your own stuff into it and make it your dance.' And that's what makes for a wonderful dance."

"Wow," I sigh, looking forward to being on the cutting edge for once in my life, dancewise.

"If you go to a studio as I have and take advanced ballroom dance, into international or American style, it's very rigid. You step here, you put your weight there, it's all a wonderful thing, but there's no act of the artist—there's no chance to freestyle on that."

"I'm afraid of ballroom because everyone has that arched back."

"It's not really arched, it's just looks that way. It is wonderful dancing. If you ever danced it, you'd really enjoy it, because you're trained. The lady becomes such a good dancer, she just knows what to do, and the guys can lead quite well too. So it has its advantages. But it's not a thing you'd want to take on as a social thing."

"Right, I think Cajun is the funnest thing. People are having fun, not miserable."

"It's a fun thing. You can wear anything, do anything. It's a unique style of dance."

"The opposite of ballroom," I reply.

"The only dance that's like Cajun to me, except it's very rigid, is West Coast Swing. There you have a lot of great dancers, the cutting edge too. It's wonderful to watch a good set of dancers, because they're always playing with each other. Sonny Watson is *fantastic* for that. He's an artist, there's no doubt about it."

"I wish I could do West Coast Swing."

"How long have you tried?"

"Not the five years it will take me."

"You've got to give it at least eighteen months! For eighteen months, you've got to do West Coast Swing and nothing but West Coast Swing."

"I know, but the trouble with West Coast Swing is then they do it to everything else. They do it to tango!"

"That's what I was going to say next."

"They have no respect!" I cry.

"No respect," he agrees with mock sadness. "You do West Coast Swing to cha-cha, you do West Coast Swing to fox-trot. Okay."

"Sonny Watson told me he does West Coast to tango."

"He does it to everything. We took Argentine tango one time; when it first came in Sonny was teaching. And I watched him, in some little bar in Glendale; he was trying to do tango to two-step, cowboy style. And it was fun to watch him play with this stuff and see how he could work it. He's a very magical person, Sonny."

"Well, everything is in everything now," I say. "I mean, Glendale is like the hub of some kind of incredible dance creativity, it's into salsa, it's into West Coast Swing, it's into the two-step. The Cajun thing has a lot of brilliant things that nobody else does."

"Cajun borrows from everybody. It's how it started. Cajun started after World War Two that I can remember, or so they told me about. The Cajuns were isolated in the bayou, they couldn't move around, they lived out there, they didn't know anything about what was going on. They saw swing, they liked it, but when they went back to the bayou, they're were no swing bands. They did have these French reels and jigs, so they started using swing steps and swing techniques on this old-type dancing. And the footwork had to match it because you can't use swing footwork for this stuff, so they ended up with this crazy dance."

"Well, I hope my book is a document of this era in the dance world. I think the kids all fell in love with Jim Carrey doing that East Coast Swing in *The Mask*."

"Oh, yeah," he remembers.

"It made a big dent on the kids. Kids want to dance like that."

"Well, I'm glad they do. It's a good way to meet people. The people in Pasadena Ballroom Dance when I was there who later became my dance buddies are a good group of people and a lot of things went on with that group. Dancers are a strange breed of people; most of the ones that I have dealt with are usually of higher intellect. Usually the men are engineers for some reason; it's not necessarily an artistic thing, it's just something they like to do—I'm talking about couple dancing, not freestyle nightclub dancing. This is a group of people who seems to be at a little higher level, most of us have some college, and they seem to have at least one or two marriages under their belts."

"So they don't want to exactly get married, but they want to have fun."

"They want to have fun and they enjoy it, they enjoy the challenges of it, they enjoy learning this type of thing—it's no different than golf, bowling, or whatever it is. It's just that now you do it as a couple."

"Right," I say. "You do it with different people, so you get to have the thrill of all these different people. But you don't have to be married to them."

"You don't have to be and you don't have to have an affair,

but the thing about this is, it's a way that people meet all over the world, in England and Germany this is the chief way people meet. And I think there's a lot to it, the compatibility factor, the attractiveness, the enjoyment of it. You're meeting among friends, which is the best way to meet. The only way people meet normally is at work. Work can be a good spot but it can limit you quite a bit; at a dance you can meet *anybody* out there. And at a dance there are all sorts of people to meet, it's just wonderful, the variety of people who come to these dances. One of the people I was dancing with Friday night was a psychologist, another was a physician. It's a lot of fun."

"It's an old-fashioned civilized way, the etiquette is all stated," I say.

"Yes, the function is, everybody learns their part, people work toward a goal. If I know that you come to these dances and you've put time into it, work into it, and effort into it, I like that. I mean, it already says something about your character to me. Now many times, I'm sure it's happened to you, I walk into one of these dances and a girl says, 'Oh, I know how to dance,' and she can't dance a step. And she wonders why she sits in the corner all night long. Because none of the other guys is going to dance with her, I mean, we dance with the gals who have put the time and the effort in."

"That's right."

"There are different styles of dance for everybody; there's an almost infinite number. For me, I got into the Cajun because it's so lowdown, a lot of fun, and I seem to like that type of music. I've also gone into the old-time dancing. I like the Victorian-era dancing, but there's Regency, there's Colonial, there's Revolution, and there's ragtime—there are all sorts of people who like this type of dancing as well. But here you have to learn not only the dance, but also the etiquette of the time. Because you must reflect some of the etiquette to do this type of dancing."

Basically in real life Bert does "property management," which means he works alone all week long. "So dancing is a way I can get to socialize. I've got two cats and I can talk to those two cats all week long."

He continues, "The Victorian dancing is to me a wonderful dance." He's a Taurus, conservative. "To me freestyle dancing is an abomination."

"An abomination?"

"For me, you have to learn to do the dances. Scottish country dancing is a dance I also do. Thursday evening there are classes."

"I want to see this," I say. "It's even *more* than partner dancing."

"What you have here is a group of people enjoying each other's company, and we begin to know each other as a *group*—we all dance as a group. It's a little bit like square dancing, which I don't know anything about."

"I like the big band dances, and Pasadena Ballroom Dance has a big band twice a year. I went to one ragtime ball and really enjoyed it. But you know, there's only so much you can do."

"All the dances we do are foreign dances . . . the ballroom, they're all from Europe, but this country is the one that invented the fox-trot, and here we're not even doing it. And the worst criticism I have is for swing—you watch these old movies, these black people doing this wonderful swing. When you think of the awful stuff they do now . . . they can't even get out and do their own dance that they invented. They invented one of the greatest dances in the world today, East Coast Swing, and they threw it away. Just threw it away. What kind of a dumb society does that?"

"It is a shame and a sin," I agree, since I hate hip-hop with a vengeance.

"It's awful hard to show people dancing and you almost have to have a posed position to do it right!"

We talk about how dancing will keep you young. "They say as long as you keep on dancing, you'll never get that geriatric walk, but I've known a few people who have actually died on the dance floor!'

"You do?"

"Oh, yeah. Well, one guy died doing West Coast. He wanted to go that way and he did."

"Who was this?

"Oh, some fellow down at Let's Dance L.A., he had some beautiful young blonde he was dancing with and he ticked off right there. I don't think he even stopped the dancing. He just died."

He then remarks that he's got to take more two-step lessons because he's got property in the boondocks, close to Fresno. The only dancing is in remote country bars, so his two-step chops have to be upgraded.

What a checkered life he lives. Maybe he too will one day die not in bed an old man, but on the dance floor, having mastered West Coast with a beautiful young blonde.

As I left the flamboyantly and robustly alive Cajun dance, I felt as though maybe one of these days, I'll go to Louisiana myself, see what the people are like, the ones besides my relatives. I have relatives, my sister who's been there tells me, who spend all year waiting for the shrimp and then fill up truckloads with them and take them to markets. Their house has water marks inside from the floods.

Being half Jewish, with the tragic, long, and fairly romantic and maniacal history that I feel from it pressing in on me every day, it's nice to know I have half of me that's just out for a *bon temps.* Not too big on Jesus or philosophy or any of these new-fangled or ancient ways people have to wreck their lives with.

But really, I like both sides of my background so much, I have a split personality. One side (my left, my heart) is the Cajun desire to let the good times roll and call everyone *cher,* and the other side (my right, my brain) knows the sadness of history, the seriousness of the mind, the distance and perspective of a people who were always outsiders. Even in the paradise of the War Memorial Hall, knowing it's only *fais-dodo.*

5

Learning Ballroom Dance with the
Amazing Stevens Sisters of Pasadena

Most everyone who learns to dance in L.A. begins at Pasadena Ballroom Dance because it is there that people who never danced a step in their life and don't want to look too much like fools feel most comfortable. It's in Pasadena, which after all is almost anonymous, almost incognito, almost out of town (except if you live in Pasadena), and going there on the oldest L.A. freeway is like driving away somewhere for a vacation. Pasadena has always been a place trying to get out of being too close to Hollywood. A place of kindly little old ladies (like the one who outstripped the guy in the Jan and Dean song), of families bent not on riches but rather on raising children to be ready to work for the Rose Parade. It's a place where they would have a rose parade and where every year, they have it again.

It's a place where the old money went from the rest of America, where those vast fortunes, like the Gambles (of Procter &) and the Wrigley of gum fame, felt safe. They felt themselves to be in a California that would never be demeaned by the tawdriness of that other part of the city. In Hollywood people might be able to dance and they might be real writers and the actors might be professional as hell, but they were not—I repeat *not*—welcome in the Pasadena where it's safe today to take ballroom dancing.

I mean, you'd take ballroom dancing in Pasadena because you'd expect that the people there probably still had ballrooms and probably still did the waltz!

Pasadena is not sexy. It's something other than that, it's not Hollywood and it never *wants* to be!

That's what's so sexy about it.

On the Stevenses' street, it's shady, it's beautiful, it's old, and I am not disappointed by where they've asked me to meet them, as I would be if they turned out to do interviews from some hideous modern building with too much air-conditioning.

This is a family that's open but cozy and no wonder the Pasadena veneer is so stiff, it's to protect the sweet and the vulnerable in a day and age when those two qualities are regarded as weird unnecessary relics like the appendix. Or like the waltz itself.

The Stevens sisters, Tami and Erin, are daughters of parents who are still married, and who actually *help* at the classes, punching tickets, taking money, *and* showing up at the dances, sitting at a quaintly decorated table, like the one where chaperones sit at a high school prom giving advice to lovelorn students trying to become "a couple." A magical friendliness having nothing to do with Hollywood glamour or California hip permeates the whole place and makes those who never danced before, little by little, begin the magical process of being As One with the Music.

"I want to invent a romance," I tell them. "Can you tell me about the typical people who meet here? Not that someone would necessarily think he/she is going to meet anyone, especially in this day and age. It's so hard to meet anyone that it's hard to *want* to meet anyone. You think everybody's got to be crazy, the whole world is bad. But in partner dancing you are at least agreeing to this dance, in this formal situation. Because you are both in the student position, it's fun. It's like going to school, so it's more flirty."

"It's true," Erin replies. "It's a great way to get to know somebody. It's safe because you get to know someone in a class situation. Right off the bat, your arms are around each other, so you're feeling closer . . . and yet you can decide how close you want to get. I mean, if you don't want to go out for coffee with him afterward, you don't have to. You can spend six weeks getting to know him pretty well in class."

"Who would be the typical person who's coming to Pasadena Ballroom—young, twenties, thirties?"

"We've always had a big variety, we've always had everything from college students to young professionals, to people up to their seventies who just want to polish up again or learn for the first time."

"And how long have you been doing this?"

"For fifteen years. I think it's amazing, it goes so fast."

"So your sister has been in the business for fifteen years too?"

"Yes, Tami and I started the business together. Our family is very close. I was a dance major at UC Irvine, doing choreography, ballet, and jazz, and I hurt my knees. I discovered that the only kind of dancing I could do was ballroom, so I actually worked my way through college, teaching at different ballroom studios down in the Orange County area.

"Tami, at the same time, was at Pasadena City College and she was taking the social dance class just for fun. Eventually she became president of their social dance club and began putting on parties for the dancers, getting to the fun aspect of it.

"When I graduated, I moved back home. I had a lot of students who still wanted private lessons, but I was no longer affiliated with the studios or making the drive, and Tami had just suffered Prop Thirteen, which cut all the funding for social activities in colleges, so her classes had been taken away. So we were sitting at lunch one day with my parents and Tami said, 'Well, maybe we ought to teach.'

"And my father said, 'Oh, I just saw this building which had a for rent sign.' So the family went and we stood on the doorstep of Vassa Temple; I guess it was a church of sorts, a Swedish temple. A woman came down and said it was for rent. We looked at the building, and on her doorstep we said, 'Well, why don't we do a six-week series, and how about teaching fox-trot, waltz, swing, cha-chas, and rumba?' So we hand-printed fliers, gave them out to our relatives and acquaintances, and at the end of six weeks, kind of looked at each other and thought, shall we do this again? and decided to do it one more time. . . . And in the course of that second round, we had about twenty students. Sixteen were relatives."

"We had to have twenty-five to pay the rent," Mrs. Stevens inserted.

"By the end of the second week, a writer from the *L.A. Times* came in and sat at the back and watched the classes and wrote this article."

With that, she brought out a laminated article from Miv Shav's column in *Home* magazine, which used to be a nice section of the *Los Angeles Times*, and Shav's column was so seductive and original, she could do anything.

"Once that came out, it changed our life, because we had to get serious after that. We had to decide on a name for the business and get a phone number. Our phone rang off the hook from people who called the newspaper, got her number, and then called us."

"So what do you think you would have done if this hadn't happened?"

"Oh, I think we were both having fun, but we both had other jobs and I think we might have left it at that."

"So publicity just blasted you out of the water."

"It made us get serious, it made us decide whether we really wanted to do this or not, and we decided it really was what we wanted to do."

"So this was February twenty-six, nineteen eighty-four. So now it's lucky there's two sisters, because you're both teaching different places each night."

"Originally we taught together. For years we taught together, I did the man's part, I wore pants every night. Then finally our business got big enough and we had enough people that we had brought up and they were good enough to help us, so we could then split and each teach in our own building. We can both teach everything."

"I'm trying to do West Coast Swing now. I don't know if I'll ever be able to do it."

"Every dance calls for its own personality."

"So what would be a good couple for a romance, a girl from Cal Tech?"

Just then, Tami enters and now, with their mother and father, the whole family of Pasadena Ballroom Dance, complete with their dog, Farley Granger Stevens, is present.

"We've had over four hundred fifty marriages. And just yesterday someone called and said that a couple had met at Catalina from Minnesota and they're getting married. They were both from Minnesota but had never met each other before but at Catalina they met and now they're a couple."

I knew that Pasadena Ballroom Dance had sponsored this huge swing camp at Catalina, and several people, including my childhood friend Janie, had gone, looking forward to it with mad abandon.

"How many people went to Catalina?"

"Eight hundred something?"

"And you did all the business too?"

"Everything. It was unbelievable."

"It's so hard to do business and art, in my experience."

"Well, fortunately our business allows us to do our art, so we love what we do. But unfortunately, we probably don't get out to play as much as we used to, because we're dancing so much. A movie sounds good on a night off. I remember fifteen years ago, when every night we were out dancing at a club. . . ."

Their own dances at the church on Walnut are really fun (I went the weekend before this interview).

"The first, third, and fourth Saturday of every month, you can come to Pasadena Ballroom Dance. But so many of the hotels have small bands, and a lot of the clubs have small bands that you don't think of as dance bands, but there are little dance floors with generally danceable music."

"What I hate is when you think you're going to dance to 'Long Ago and Far Away' and then it turns out to be this long jazz riff that goes on forever."

"Right. We always tell the bands who come to play for us, play the songs short. Usually when they come they play a long version, but then I say, 'Play the songs short. Our people are singles, they want to dance with a lot of other people.' That, coupled with a long break between songs, can be really awkward. If you're standing there and you've asked someone to dance and the song finishes, you're thinking, Okay, I might want to dance another one. But if you're out there with no music, no nothing, and you're wondering—"

"However, if you hated the dance," Tami breaks in, "it's definitely time for water!"

"These dances, they seem to be building momentum. Pretty soon are they going to be every night of the week?"

"No, I think we've maxed out on days of the week because

Fridays are now our only night off, plus one Saturday a month."

"You seem to be dancing every minute."

Tami begins answering my earlier question about romance. "Two people from Minnesota—Rusty and Simon, she was in our classes, she's a tap dancer now. We hired her to teach tap to a swing dancer from England and now she's moved to England. She met him in June in Catalina—she'd barely met him prior to that—they rowed over on the boat together, and even on the boat you could see, they just clicked. They sat together and never stopped talking, they were just enthralled with each other. Then at the dances they were glued to each other, we all saw it happening. And then she gave up basically everything that she had here, a great job, Disney Animation Studios, and she wrote a book on tap."

"Oh, I know her, she used to go to the Atlas, which was such a fun place when that band was there."

"Yeah, she's friends with the man you came with. Well she's gone, she went the beginning of August—the first few days were kind of rocky, but now they're living together and they're just thrilled. Just like they found the right one."

"Well, you guys seem to be on angels' wings of luck."

"To be honest, Dad is the matchmaker. My father *always* has had this knack for looking at people and saying, 'Oh, this would be a good match.' He denies it. He sits at the desk and people pour their hearts out to him and he suggests someone, then he introduces them, and the next thing you know, they're married. In fact, he's even been the best man, giving the bride away, to someone he did this with."

"The thing is, you guys provide a place where people are not uptight and crazy. A lot of dance classes are very intense."

"It's very social. I mean, they learn a lot, but it's more relaxed. You know, after class we play a few songs and in breaks we play songs. People have an opportunity to relax and really get to know each other. I think it does provide a nice environment.

"But anyway, this particular one, she had a couple of different men in class in whom she was very interested—and vice versa—and she poured her heart out to Dad about every one of them, but she finally settled on one. She had talked to Dad so much that she asked him to please give her away."

"So you guys are always buying wedding shower gifts?"

"It's so funny, the perspective of being the teacher in class. You watch the rotation as you change partners, and I don't know if we've inherited it from Dad, but I swear we can look down and say, 'That person, when they hit this partner, that's going to be a match.' The next thing you know, they're leaving together, going out for coffee. You can just tell it all, you can see the way the line's going.

"You know, I met my husband that way. My husband was a student at Cal Poly Pomona, part of a graduating class I had been hired to teach to dance at a graduation party. I took one of our teaching assistants, who happened to know my husband, and when we arrived it was the worst job I ever taught, nobody wanted to dance. As a teacher, sometimes you are brought into a situation where people are expecting a dance lesson and looking forward to it, and sometimes you're brought in and it's the last thing they want to do. This was a nightmare job. Jim arrived late, he just came to help clean up the party, but I grabbed him out of the crowd and said, 'Help me demonstrate.' When the rest of the crowd saw him doing it then they got into it.

"So everybody got up to dance and it turned the job around. After that, he followed me home, came to our dance classes, and then we started dating."

"He was so shy," Erin adds. "He would peek in the door, most often after class he would come in and take her out for coffee. . . . That was a long time ago. They went together for six years."

"Well, that's good, you didn't make any sudden lurch. You didn't go to England and give up your life."

"My husband, Scott, came with a girl to class—this was probably ten years ago or so and I was dating someone else who wasn't part of the classes—so I got to know both him and his girlfriend as they danced in class for a while. When he broke up with her, he was kind of around for a long time and we thought he was an excellent dancer. We hired him to work with us for a good year. Then I put him on the performance crew troupe which Tami and I are a part of and I paired Tami and Scott for a tango number. That did it, what can I say—we were both seeing two different people and we both kind of broke up with them at the same time and we both just started to hang out together, and probably . . ."

"Two to four years after that," Tami says, "they were married. Tango."

"That's *great*. I don't think the lindy is that sexy."

"Some of our guys are surprisingly acrobatic; in the lindy class, they are really great."

"Isn't it great that the swing is coming back?"

"Erin taught lindy hop for years and years and years, and nobody even knew what the word was, we had to talk so hard to say what it was, and now everybody's saying it."

"Frankie Manning?"

"Well, he lives in New York but he teaches around the world. He's teaching here for us. He started off as a kid when he was about six years old. His mom told him, Honey, you'll never be a dancer, you're so stiff! And that became a life mission to him. At the age of sixteen, he was dancing at the Savoy as one of the top dancers when Herbert Whiting approached him and said he was putting together a troupe called Whiting's Lindy Hoppers and he'd like to have him in the troupe. So at sixteen, he basically ran away, because his mom said 'no way' to tour South America, tour Europe, have these experiences, and be a part of the William Morris Agency."

"This was in the heart of the Depression," Tami reminds us, "and this team of dancers was making big bucks and dancing all around the world."

"And I guess after the war years," Erin continues, "the era changed and partner dancing changed."

"The fifties—the twist!"

"Frankie tried to start his own troupe in the fifties, but basically there wasn't the calling for it, so he went to work at the post office and basically retired from dancing.

"So, in nineteen eighty-two or eighty-three I met my dance partner, Steve Mitchell, at Pasadena City College. We were tap dance partners, then we became disco partners—disco was big—and then we thought we'd like to explore other styles. Well, big bands were back in in the early eighties. There was the Bob King band and Bill Davies . . . Basically it was a period when big band dancing was back and we were going to these bands every night. They would always have dance contests and most of the time it was a cha-cha, don't ask me why, but that's what was in. Steve and I *really* started dancing the cha-cha because we made big bucks winning contests.

"One night one of the bands, Bob King's band, said we're going to play down at the Miramar and why don't you come, we're having a contest. We thought, 'easy money,' and went down there. It was a swing contest—and we'd never done swing—but the band was playing something like 'Lady Be Good' and Steve just started doing what came naturally from his soul. He was twisting around, went into the splits, and at one point he jumped over my head. I would just twist around him and we won the contest.

"And at the end of it, we thought we'd better learn swing, so we started looking around here for what we *felt* we wanted to do. West Coast Swing was very big, but nobody was doing up-tempo swing, so we would get together and practice. It was about the time that Tami and her boyfriend were very into the Marx Brothers. They brought us home this footage from *A Day at the Races* and they said, 'Look at this, there's some swing dancing in this!' Steve looked at it and said, 'That's what I want to do.'

"So this was our daily agenda. We would start out watching the tape, try and imitate the movement, and we would learn the steps, backwards and forwards. We would do the steps, the lifts, everything. Then at one point my father brought home a *Life* magazine that he found that had lindy hop on the cover—it was August twenty-four, nineteen forty-six—but anyway, it was all lindy hop and listed the names of these dancers who all lived in New York.

"So Steve and I had this mission to go to New York. With a phone book under an arm—we actually spent time in the library ringing these phone numbers and then we went to New York, sat in a phone booth, went through the entire phone book—we called every name from that magazine. There were Willa Mae Ricker and Leon James—there were tons of them listed, it's a very popular name in New York, Leon James—but anyway we went through all the names and nobody had a clue what we were talking about.

"Then hours later, dimes later, we tried dance studios and asked, 'Are there any original lindy hoppers still alive?' and one pointed us in the direction of Al Mins, who had danced in the same troupe as Frankie and was one of the original guys. We spent that summer studying with Al Mins, who couldn't tell us what the basic was, but could teach us more aerials and some of the flash steps.

"Two years later Al Mins passed away. We were still on the search for other dancers, and I met a man who was a writer for *The Atlantic Monthly* doing an article on California and West Coast Swing and the revival of this East Coast, lindy hop–type swing. He was searching for names and somewhere in the midst of it all the name Frankie Manning came up. I said I'd give him a call, and I called him—he was in the phone book. He said he would meet with us 'next time you're in New York,' but he was very adamant that he did not teach and was fully retired.

"So Steve and I booked another trip to New York and he agreed to meet us at a party and watch us dance. Okay, he said, he would teach us, and we were in town for about two weeks learning from him, we worked with him every day."

"He took them to his *home*," Tami points out.

"Yeah, he was really inspired by our look. We danced on his carpet and then he took us out every night. It was just Frankie week after week. He took us to Harlem and showed us the Apollo Theatre and where the Savoy used to be. He really gave us the tour. He couldn't *count* the rhythm, but basically could show us what lindy hop was supposed to look like."

"And that's what started it off," Tami says.

"We're credited with being the ones to bring him out of retirement," Erin agrees, "for inspiring him to teach again. We were the first ones to hire him and actually bring him out here to teach.

"And now he's never home. He's just, I don't know, at various swing camps. In nineteen ninety-two he won a Tony for his choreography for *Black and Blue*, the show on Broadway. The next morning he called Erin and *thanked* her because he felt that she was so instrumental in bringing him out, in making him dance again. So we really have a kinship with the man."

"You can imagine, you can imagine!" Erin trills. "He's such a sweet man, humble, he sends us birthday cards and anniversary cards. He wouldn't miss an occasion, for as busy as he is, he never misses maintaining the friendships."

"In dancing, some people are loved in it and some people aren't."

"Well, Frankie is so beloved by people around him."

"Orlando, the tango master, is that way. When he's around everyone behaves well, but the minute he goes, everyone reverts to type."

I follow another thought and ask, "Did you see that movie *Swing Kids?*"

"From a dancer's perspective," Erin responds, "it was a typical thing. They hired someone who really couldn't dance but he had the insight to hire the right people to be underneath him. So they had some great choreographers on the set, but then they were given nondancers—so all the elements didn't come together. It couldn't have been great. It was a very depressing film and in the middle there were these dance scenes. It was very hard because the dance is such a high and happy thing, and there'd be a great dance scene, followed by such a letdown in the film. For me, it didn't work—I would have liked more dancing, less violence."

"In Hollywood," Tami moans, "they cut so much of the dancing."

"That's why I loved *Dirty Dancing.* They didn't care about the plot at all!"

"So often they show the people dancing from the waist up or the audience," Erin says, agreeing with her sister. "People I know were so disappointed with *The Mambo Kings* because we had so many people who went and such good dancers who were on the set and . . ."

"Apparently, from what I heard, they had to make Armand Assante look better than everybody, and since he was worse than everybody, they had to *hide* everybody."

"We were extras on a film set where the stars—they tried to teach them to dance, but they couldn't—were on this moving thing rigged to move them in waltz tempo back and forth. They just held each other and we danced around it."

"I think of you two as working too hard all day on this business to be extras."

"We *do* work all day," Mrs. Stevens says. "I mean, this phone rings all day long, constantly leaving messages."

"We teach privates all day," Tami says. "Erin had two today, but normally we try to take a week off between—one solid week off, in August—but obviously you don't turn off the phone, you still have to answer phone calls. So, in a sense you're still working during the day. But then, our mailing list is gigantic. We have over eight thousand names and I have to keep track of all that on the computer."

"It's great that you're so successful. You know, apparently there's going to be another *Dirty Dancing* movie."

"I will say that the lindy hop thing is a side thing that's happened for us, but our ballroom classes have *always* happened for us, I mean, this is what kind of has set us apart, and our ballroom is our base."

"And the point is," Mrs. Stevens is quick to add, "it's *social* ballroom, it's not international, so everybody gets to use it, quickly."

"And you can have a regular person's comprehension," I add, thinking just how important this is in my case.

"*Anybody* can walk off the street and generally 'get it,'" Tami agrees.

Acknowledging their contribution to the dance, I add, "And Pasadena, in everybody's minds, it's just old ladies and gentility and ballroom dancing, beautiful old houses and the past and the Green Hotel and . . ."

"Right, right"—Tami and Erin nod knowingly, in unison—". . . mansions."

Driving away from the Stevenses' perfectly Pasadena old house, I wondered what it might have been like growing up in the City of Widows. A place where in 1930 the census said 75 percent of the population was almost entirely widowed; women whose husbands had written into their wills that they could never remarry or they'd lose everything.

Salsa with Albert Torres and Renée Victor

In the fabulous Broadway Deli, a new landmark on the Third Street Promenade, not too far from his new Sunday classes at the Ash Grove on the Santa Monica Pier, I meet with Albert Torres. He seems to be a mild-mannered man dressed in white, except when he dances, at which time *anything* can happen.

In my experience, all salsa dancers, unless they are in partnership with another dance teacher, *hate* all other dance teachers, if not all other dancers anywhere near as good as themselves. It is as though being bitter is a Latin style. I've heard people say that one teacher looks too much at their feet when they dance. That another forces his partner into "disrespectful" positions. That an old-style salsa dancer who dances only on the "two" looks constipated because all he seems to be doing is grinding his heels into the floor as if in some kind of digestive pain. I've heard a lot of stuff, each camp has its own flag and enemy but really, in salsa, the dance is so basically easy. I've seen certain people able to teach someone enough to pick up the step, the whole *look* of salsa/mambo, in half an hour, like East Coast Swing.

Oh, and that's another thing. The mambo/salsa thing, which we see a little of in the movie *Dirty Dancing* (my favorite dance movie), the old-style thing about the mambo, that you had to dance it on the "two." The two is the second beat, which in the olden days used to be played by a clave (percussive sticks)— which in those days people could *hear.* Today, due to improvements, you can't hear the two, so everyone dances on whatever they want except percussionists, who are able to hear everything, but who even so usually can't dance that well.

In Los Angeles today, there are a lot of places to go Latin dancing and oddly enough, even though it is mixed up in our minds with the dancers in *West Side Story*, in most dance situations, getting wounded is the last thing on anyone's mind. Dancers have a sort of Piscean self-esteem, a sort of "let's go out every night and feel the magic and let's do it again and again."

Once anyone ties themselves to any partner dance, their life of criminal behavior has to go. Dancing with a partner requires social skills that have nothing to do with violence, but the opposite—peace on earth and goodwill to the dance place. Partner dancing is a cultured act; once anyone gets into it, they are a step up from violence, they are in civilized survival skills training. A man who can dance with his wife, his girlfriend, or his mother is a man women will protect. Of course, in fact, there are really great dancers who use their chops to acquire women who pay for everything. Gigolos, they used to be called, and still are. But then those women have a lot of money to spend on their own amusement, and money to get their hearts broken. One of the best dancers I ever saw recently died of AIDS because he just couldn't keep from selling drugs, being thrown in jail, and worse came to worse.

Social dance scenes have always been a mixture of the barely contained criminal element, the very rich, and in between, middle-class dancers who just want a partner, the night, and the music. Me, I have no idea how someone who was a great dancer, especially Latin, would get the mind-set of getting something for nothing. When it's so hard to learn these steps it would be obvious that to do anything well you have to pay in sweat and tears.

Anyway, Albert Torres right now is the west side of L.A.'s leading salsa instigator. He throws great dances, he teaches everywhere, and he's very patient with beginners, letting them dance on whatever beat they can muster up. A great time is likely whenever he's around, because seeing him dance, you just swoon, he's so great.

I propose to Albert that salsa is a great dance for people who really want to learn how to move.

"Well, look at the benefits," he says. "The benefits are you really feel good about yourself, and sexy, you get through some of your issues from childhood and the whatnot of getting out there. I love the statement that all of us are born unique, but most of us wind up dying copies—copies because we emulate a certain individual, their stuff, and that's what we live for. 'I want to be that rock-and-roll star, I want to be that dancer, I want to be Donald Trump.' The reality is you have your own originality, you were born with that, and we can learn from all other experiences. Even in the dance world, you can learn from my steps and Laura's steps, everyone's steps."

"I'm focusing on the classes, the learning, and how long it takes you," I say. "The classes are the most fun, because you get to be in that state of learning; being with the opposite sex, and being in school and learning. It's a great way to meet people.

"Have you done any other kinds of dancing?" I ask him.

"Early on I worked with Chubby Checker. I danced the Hustle professionally for a long, long time. I did the twist and the limbo—that was when I really could do it, in the early seventies, when Chubby Checker came back. I was born and raised in New York and Puerto Rico."

"A Puerto Rican dancer—whoever heard of that?"

"It's a myth, believe me. My brother, he lives in Puerto Rico now, he's been taking dancing for about a year. I'm going to take him to all these clubs and check out what he's learned. I'd take him to the Sportsman's Lodge on a Friday night. I wouldn't go there usually, but I'd take him to the Mayan on a Saturday night."

"What's it like? I've never been there."

"It's a zoo, a zoo. There are probably twelve hundred people there, all young, all getting drunk. Mostly in their twenties."

"Well, I think salsa is great because the entry level seems easy. On your first lesson you think you know it, but then, after three months . . ."

"You start thinking, and it's 'Oh, no!' "

"So Albert, how long have you been teaching?"

"Officially, oh, about three years. But prior to that, like, fifteen years ago. Then I stopped teaching and I got sober. Initially when I got sober, I danced. I used to dance sober dances at the retail clerks union, but I stopped dancing for about ten years because I was tired of the competitive level. I used to go to the Jockey Club in the marina, it was just Hustle and disco. I stopped dancing salsa for about ten years, then close to nine years ago I decided to go back to my roots. I had all these movies and a collection of music, and it was time to stop hiding it and hiding from the scene. I decided if anyone was going to do something about it, I should do something myself."

"Yeah, you reach a certain age and realize nobody's going to take over but you."

"So I started doing some research. I'm working on becoming a musicologist. I've studied the movies, I've studied the literature. I see what I think is BS and what I think is true and I've got references of what I think is happening. I put together my own little stories of what I've learned from the history."

"Well, my favorite song is 'El Caballo Viejo,' which is on *Boleo*, the first Gypsy Kings album. The song is about how if you bet on love, it's like an old horse; it doesn't come in. And I love Julio Iglesias. I know he's a cornball, but I love him. At the end of a performance he kisses the stage—performers from Spain kiss the stage because that's why they're there. Even in high heels, a mother, after her songs, she kisses the stage, a lipstick blot on the stage. I think there's this huge Latin scene, there are so many Mexicans here, but are there Cubans, are there Latinos?"

"There are Cubans and there are Puerto Ricans. The influence now has gone a lot to the South Americas; they've really got connected. Someone like an Oscar de León, he's an incredible singer. He and other groups from South America, they're bringing their own type of sound into salsa music; it's helping the South American crowd get more into it. And the Mexicans, they're beginning to enjoy it and are getting away from the cumbia and the carbarlita a little bit. I have a lot of Mexicans who go to my club, the Sportsman's Lodge, that'll be four to five hundred people."

"The funniest thing happened to me at the Sportsman's Lodge. It was a year or so ago, they had this Latin dance contest—they always seemed to have the hokiest dance contests. All the judges were mambo teachers from some Arthur Murray–type places and all the dancers were wild salsa dancers, so the people who won were like the ones with nine thousand dollars' worth of lessons. But the people the crowd wanted to win were the wild and great salsa dancers, so then there was this huge rumble, like when a soccer team loses.

"So how many people are you teaching right now?"

"The class will have fifty people at the Sportsman's Lodge, and at the Ash Grove it ranges from twenty-five to forty people, depending on the Sunday. Then I have about fifteen private clients that I teach. I also have a mailing list on computer and I guess a friend of mine has a calypso-type Web site. Today we added a page of salsa, Cajun-zydeco—if you double-click on that, it'll come up salsa. And I just got a movie yesterday, it's called *Out to Sea*. I had to audition doing a rumba, a fox-trot, a waltz, a mambo, and a swing. It stars Jack Lemmon and Walter Matthau, one of those grumpy old men movies, but now they're out on a cruise ship. They picked eight dancers to be the main dancers and twenty others filling in. We start rehearsing next week and start filming October twenty-eighth."

"That reminds me, dancing in *The Mambo Kings* was an incredible experience. I got to dance with people like Cuban Pete and his ex-wife, Meli, and see a lot of the older dancers who would dance at the Palladium—around my mom's age—and I heard all these stories, and confirmed a lot of stories."

"Was your mother a dancer?"

"My mom was an incredible dancer. She lives in Puerto Rico now and is a little overweight, but she's so light on her feet, she's an incredible dancer."

"I love to see great dancers who aren't skinny but are light on their feet. I love that—I think women should be women, for God's sake."

"She's just great to dance with. The experience of *The Mambo Kings* was, I think, that it helped, at least for the dancers in Los Angeles, to bridge the gap between the youth and some of the more mature dancers. It gave us a commonality and got us to sit down and talk and realize that we can hang out together and learn from each other and be open. Go out and dance mambo and have fun."

"Did the older dancers just hate the kids or did the kids hate the older dancers?"

"No, I think each part had responsibility for their own feelings. I think there was a block in that the older dancers thought,

'If you don't dance on two, you don't belong on the dance floor,' and the youngsters were thinking, 'Why dance on two? I'm having much more fun on this rhythm.' My philosophy is, you dance on whatever you dance on and have fun with it. As you dance more and more, and get more comfortable with it, I strongly suggest you at least learn a little bit on the two because—"

"The thing is, I can never *hear* the two!"

"That's the thing about two, you barely can hear it. I tell people, I'm teaching you to dance on one so you can have fun with it and if not, you may as well do Romanian belly dancing, you're going to leave here frustrated. My goal is, you leave here having had fun and keep coming back, we'll have you hooked. You'll learn on one, and having heard me say many many times that after you get on one, then I strongly encourage you to learn on two—that way you have the best of both worlds."

"How do you think people originally learned on two? I think the music, you could *hear* it back then in the olden days."

"I think you can hear the conga beat. It's so distinctive, anytime the conga is hitting the *bajo*—the bass drum, that's the two—that drum on the two and the six, you could hear it. But now with all the instrumentation, all the trumpets, it just gets lost."

Renée Victor's Salsa One class is filled with either beginners or people who go dancing already, at places like the Sportsman's Lodge, but want to hone their skills. Or at least they do after seeing Renée dance somewhere and learn she teaches class.

In her class, Renée teaches the Truth about dancing in public these days. How to pace yourself when the band plays too fast (as they all do because that's the rage now). How to do spins that she brought in from ballet. How, if you are the woman, to handle being led by a man from South America, who "just smashes the woman into his chest." As Renée told me last night, "The man I danced with last night, he leads with his diaphragm."

And yet sometimes Renée seems to dislike salsa and the horse it rode in on, and is critical of all the people she ever met, scorning the mere idea that these people think they can dance —when it's so obvious they're piddling amateurs. Which everybody but her, of course, is.

But then, salsa doesn't bring out the best in people unless you think temper and flair and genius are the best. Salsa is a dance of contradictions. On the one hand, you want to be "small," as people who lead you will say if you take steps that are too large. But on the other hand, you want to stagger your competition by the immensity of your intensity. You want your own smoldering pride and divine fire to consume the room, and yet you want to hardly move.

I have seen Renée Victor, when dancing salsa, bring down the house not only at some small North Hollywood nightclub like Norah's, where the people are mostly the bourgeoisie from South America, but also when the audience is very sophisticated and they just sit there, gasping.

Miranda Garrison, a wonderful dancer-choreographer who is a great tango-salsa-anything-really dancer herself, calls Renée "the Lioness." But that is too small a concept, she is bigger than just an animal. She is a person who's taken ballet and flamenco into salsa and filled it with orange flames.

In her beginner class, which she teaches when she's not out acting in movies or doing the choreography (or teaching someone like Gena Rowlands a danzón), she has both people who have never done any dancing, not even salsa, before, and people who could pass, if you didn't know too much, for okay dancers.

But when you see Renée dance, a simple thing like a "chase," this step they have in cha-cha that you do in the shine position, it's an okay little step thing. When Renée does it, it is *flooded* with the spirit of Dance and anyone the least remotely a dancer of any kind comes from miles around to make her acquaintance.

"My daughter heard I made a movie with Christopher Walken," she told me, "and she said, 'Mom, did you dance with him?'"

"I didn't even know he was a dancer," she said, "but after my daughter told me that, I asked him. I said, 'I heard you're a pretty good dancer,' and you know what he said, which is why I know he's probably great? He said, 'I used to be good, but that was a long time ago.'"

"He was great in *Pennies from Heaven*," I recalled.

"He must be good," she said. "It's only people who have no idea what dancing is who think they are great."

I didn't add, "And *you*," because we both know she thinks she's great and she *is*; no modest lily blooming unseen, with Renée around.

I would have loved seeing Renée dance with Christopher Walken, but that's the thing about the dance world, you get crushes on someone and the whole point is to dance with them. Not what I used to do as a groupie, which was spontaneous but never lasted long enough and was certainly nowhere near as good for your health. And the thing about dancing with someone is that afterward you sit down and then dance with someone else.

"Dancing is a flirtation, first of all," she once told me, back in the days when I was still trying to learn steps and couldn't follow and was just a bit of a mess. "You must know that, it's the main thing about partner dancing."

This is when I got the idea to do the book about partner dancing. I thought I would show how each dance was a flirtation, but really most people have a hard enough time just doing the dance, so looking at their partner is often enough to throw them off. But when Renée dances with someone . . . well, as Fred Astaire said about dancing with Cyd Charisse, "Once you danced with her, you *stayed* danced with."

Renée used to tell me that women sent their boyfriends to her, men who could not dance a step and never would learn how. Renée said, "I taught them to *stand* so they *looked* like great dancers."

In fact, one man I know has this fantasy that he will one day be a great dancer (and if he takes enough private lessons with Renée, it *must* come to pass), and he often looks like a great dancer. It's the way he stands, the poise she's instilled in him through dint of singular purpose. No one who's come to her embarrasses her from then on. And the truth is, I myself love dancing with him, because he just looks so perfect that for me, it's a joy. Well, dancing with this man is like being led by Renée, which is not to be sneezed at after all.

I first saw Renée Victor dance back in my Orlando days when he was teaching tango at Norah's, this warm and sweet Bolivian place in North Hollywood. I remember it was a sort of hot night and Renée came in wearing what looked to me like some sort of Japanese outfit; she even had chopsticks in her hair. And a hush fell over the place and at first I thought, "She's so old, she looks an ancient relic," and then I thought, "She's fourteen, what was I thinking?"

And this was just from the entrance; this wasn't from watching her dance.

I saw the man she was with, a tall man in a suit, take Renée over and introduce her to Orlando. I watched her shake hands with Orlando and then—I don't know how it happened—Orlando asked her to dance.

Now, it was his rule never to dance more than two dances once the class was over, or else his students would have danced the life out of him. Since I had never seen Renée there before, and apparently they had just been introduced, I couldn't imagine how she would be able to follow him, because I'd been taking the tango from Orlando for a year and I still couldn't follow him.

Nevertheless, Orlando took Renée out to the dance floor, the live bandoneon was playing some Gardel song as usual, and suddenly, well, rapture hit a major chord in this place, everyone's hearts were just in love. To see Renée dancing with Orlando, it was one of those moments when time stood still. Orlando's whole premise, like Ray Charles—the slower the better—Renée understood and brought with it this kind of trembling flicker of her foot, like a butterfly afraid to land, and yet like a butterfly in slow motion. Slower than Orlando.

And I thought she was Japanese, really, until the next time she came on a Saturday night or something and wore a red dress. When the little salsa band played everyone's favorite song, some great "El Caballo Viejo" or one of those, and she was dancing with this man in a suit, the whole place just creamed with stunned amazement because this was not just someone doing mambo, this was *art*.

Sometimes when I look at Renée today, she still strikes me as this vision of some ancient relic, a dance icon from some past civilization, thrown into our dance world to drive us all crazy and make everyone improve vastly. There is something so primal about her; I just can't help it.

On the other hand, she's fun to go shopping with, she's fun to eat sushi with, and she's fun to give books to, to talk to on the phone. She's a regular modern woman living in the regular modern world, with an ex-husband, two daughters grown up, always on the verge of getting a sitcom but never yet, so far.

When she acts in plays, she gets amazing reviews, and when she sings you think she's a divine woman. She and her ex-husband used to have a band and a musical variety series in Australia, where "we went over like a house on fire" she told me. "I never danced when I was married, not for fifteen years, except on the stage alone, because my husband, he never wanted to do any social dancing, it just broke my heart."

Renée has such passion in the way she approaches salsa that in spite of her proclivity to enjoy hugely terrible moods, when she dances she is free. People who have seen Renée dance with men she never met before, much less danced with, think she has occult powers, that she can follow anyone, that it's some magical gift.

"Well," she explains, "when I dance with a man, I *try* not to be a hindrance."

Renée has such a passion in the way she approaches salsa that when she dances, she is cleansed in the flame of youth and she becomes a girl of fourteen, dancing for the first time, flirting with her first man.

"I think if I have a native gift in partner dancing, it's my innate ability to follow. I could follow since I was a child. My father was really a very good dancer. I didn't know how good a dancer he was then, I just remember people used to always marvel at this little girl being able to follow. All throughout my life I've never had to practice with a dancer to be able to follow him. Most of the time my most admired or respected exhibitions have been totally unrehearsed. So I've always had that knack."

"Something about the way you follow," I add, enthusiastically, "makes the person who's dancing with you dance better!"

"Oh, sure—because you're not a *hindrance*. If the woman can't follow a good male dancer, she's going to be a hindrance, no question. Quite often I have to keep myself in check and not be impatient when I meet females. I just think the lead is so brutal, no one could possibly miss it, but that's because I find it so easy. I have to remember that and not be impatient; know that not everyone picks up a clue like that."

"So you came to Los Angeles . . ." I prompt her.

"Yes, I taught at various dance schools. The beauty of social dancing is that people endeavor to look pretty, it's not like ballet where you're wearing sweats and your hair's in a knot. The beauty about social dancing is that it makes people want to look pretty and elegant. Working women, whether they make modest salaries or not, will spend money on their nails, on their hair, and on their wardrobe to look beautiful when they go dancing that night.

"It's a wonderful sport, dancing is a very wonderful sport. Particularly social dancing, because it's a sport—and a skill—that you can continue to own for the rest of your life. There is no limit. A boxer has a limit, a ballerina has a limit, a tennis player has a limit, an ice skater has a limit, but people in any form of social dancing have no limit. Whether you want to go pro or whether you're a hobbyist, it's a wonderful thing.

"It's a skill that you can continue to use for the rest of your life, anywhere in the world. That's what is so wonderful about social dancing and partner dancing—in all of its forms, from two-step to country dancing, to the Spanish paso doble. And I enjoy teaching people who are serious, because they're after a skill, they're learning a skill."

"I was listening to one of the Dodgers last night, being interviewed," I say, "who said he was studying martial arts. He said it was the only thing that made his ball playing better, but that he didn't have to think about what he did."

"Sure," Renée adds, "I think dancing is the same way, because eventually you don't have to think about it, that's true."

"And," I went on, "it makes the rest of your life better too, it makes you get a public persona. What would you say is the attitude of salsa?"

"Sexuality and passion mixed with humor," Renée responds, laughing.

"Tango?"

"Sensuality and passion, of course, and elegance. It's a beautiful dance, no question about it. But it tends to make people take themselves too seriously."

"Yes, it does, doesn't it? I did it for so long, how could I have done that? I was so miserable. What about East Coast Swing?"

"East Coast Swing is just a fun aerobics, it's just frivolous and fun. All forms of dancing are very athletic, but swing is just total fun. It's like going to the gym except without the exertion and boredom of it."

"Right, you can flirt." Then I ask, "Renée, have you ever heard of a dance called Pony Swing?"

"No."

"Well with your occult ability to follow, I would love you to try to do Pony Swing. It's so fast, it's like a convoluted pretzel done to Cajun music. It's real fast, and it's so fast you can't see it."

"Well," she says, "I love Cajun music, and I'm dying to go to In Cahoots, darling, because I am a Texan. There is a country-western dance class right in North Hollywood. I teach at Madeline Clark and I know it's right near there."

"I think a lot of people are taking a lot of different classes."

"Americans are dancing maniacs, darling," Renée says. "I have worked all over the world and I know of no country that has as many dance schools as the United States. I wrote an article once in which I said that Americans are the best dancers—which they are. The reason they are is because collectively they are all races; it's not an insult to the Latins or an insult to anyone. America is comprised of all people and this compliment goes to all of them.

"There is no country that has as many dance schools. Get in your car and start driving and look. You can't go too many blocks without seeing a dance school. Americans *embrace* a new dance, number one. Number two, Americans create dance after dance after dance. When the go-go dancers were popular, there was a new dance every week—the Mashed Potato, the Jerk, the Pony, the Chicken—there was one after the other. You thought that was going to be it, it followed right on the heels of the twist, but soon after all of those dances came the Hustle. And after the Hustle, then came Moon Walking. After Moon Walking came Popping, and we don't stop. How can that be ignored? Look at all the variations in swing—you're already telling me about a swing dance I haven't heard of, which is a derivative of swing, from jitterbug to swing to the lindy. What about the Bunny Hop? What about all the dances, the Charleston even—who else in the world has all this dancing? Look what happened after *Tango Argentino* came to the United States. Have you ever seen such a burgeoning of tango teachers? Why? Because it was embraced.

"Americans are taking trips to Argentina to learn it—that's a race of people who loves to dance. It's the only country that I know of in which you can run the gamut and find everything from a good Charleston dancer to a Popper and everything in between. You have your Latin specialists, your tango specialists, your tap dancers, your lindy . . . And another reason is affluence. Americans can afford to go and take lessons."

"And they're healthy, they've got energy," I point out. "And they don't mind being the worst person in the room" (speaking from personal experience).

"No!" Renée agrees wholeheartedly. "They're not embarrassed by this and that. And they are willing to go and pay to be taught to do something the right way. But then, there are so many of us who just take things up by watching. But any way you slice it, Americans are lovers of dancing. They love to dance."

But really, for me, salsa is so hard and difficult, I just don't know what to do, especially in Los Angeles right now, where all the really proficient dancers, like Toni Basil, live. All the really inside people are learning salsa now and there are huge dances in downtown L.A. For instance, at the Mayan Theater, where Albert tells me 1,200 people go, it's wall-to-wall salsa.

The whole thing with salsa, it seems to me, is control of your feet and your torso. The thing is, the young people never look as great as the older dancers because even though they're gorgeous they lack the expertise and control—which is the same in all dances, I suppose. You have to move your feet so fast, they have to move so exactly on the beat, and yet you have to look like you don't care all that much really, like it's just the music moving you to such exquisite excess.

Salsa, for those who don't know, is a Cuban dance. It's a dance that only rich or idle people with shady pasts can do because they alone have the time and money to learn this dance.

Tiffany Brown's East Coast Swing Class
at the Hollywood Derby

It was such a great idea I was afraid it might become a chain. The Derby, the swing bands, the "free" swing dance classes, and Tiffany Brown, except that with Tiffany Brown, there's only one. And on the nights she's not teaching, nobody comes to a "free" lesson.

"Oh, they only come when I teach because of the band," she modestly disclaims. "It's the band they like."

Except when Tiffany is teaching, there is an atmosphere of "We are in the right place at the right time, this is *it*!" She is part of this trend right now, for kids who are into the old cars, the vintage clothes, the cigars, the old music, two-tone shoes—a thing that translates at the Viper Room on the Sunset Strip to Martini Night. There, on Thursday nights, when the DJ is called the Sultan of Swoon, the World's Most Sophisticated and Hippest get to hear Glenn Miller's "String of Pearls" and watch the fruits of Tiffany's lessons—kids who've had one lesson or two or three charge out there with a partner and holy Toledo, they're dancing.

What's really funny are these older men, in their seventies, who wear yellow polo shirts and white pants and white shoes. I've seen several of these guys, out at the Viper Room, dancing with these girls with green hair who want someone to twirl them who knew how in the past. It's a mixture of punk and the Real Thing.

Punk was an expensive trend; you can't be a punk and have to work in a bank. The people who were punk—even though they thought anarchy was their basis—have discovered, as they grow older, that "class" is the Thing. One of those guys started a big swing orchestra and it's on the road as I write this. The punkers were too smart to stay punk when they could play actual music. They want Class.

On to the, well, the elegant swing dance couple. The lesson for the elegant swing dance couple is on Wednesday night at the Derby, taught by Tiffany Brown, the Angel of Swing.

Tiffany is the angel who stands patiently, greeting kids in their twenties who have never danced before, who expect, for the "free" hour-long lesson (which costs $5), to learn enough to go dance on a dance floor in public to a live band.

"Oh, okay," she seems to sigh, each Wednesday at 8:00 P.M. when there's no one there and she could, in fact, think, "Well, maybe they're not coming, maybe swing is out." But by 8:15, the place has maybe forty people in it, and by 8:45 it could have seventy. By 9:00 the fanciest swing dancers from all over L.A. are likely to arrive (if they like the band at the Derby) and they enter in their two-tone shoes and great retro outfits: the girls in flying skirts, the guys' hats even with feathers—they just explode for the eyes of the beginners.

But one thing about East Coast Swing: your grandmother could learn it on a cruise from an instructor in ten minutes, or the basics anyway. And nobody in East Coast goes complaining, "These kids today, they don't even know the *basics*!" In swing dancing you hunch up and move fast; the only thing you could possibly do wrong is have balletic posture.

Anyway, the kids arrive—girls in long skirts with their belly buttons showing below short little *Friends*-type thrift store sweaters with short sleeves; guys who are the most obvious heteros in ugly clothes and terrible, terrible shoes.

This is the only dance class on earth where Doc Martens are

considered just fine. Doc Martens are those heavy combat boot things from England, for those of you with no punk rockers in your family; they are the shoes that make kids look like refugees landing at Ellis Island, and they cost $100. When the guys get good, then they branch out and buy bowling shoes, which are not only two-tone, but have suede soles like dancer's shoes should. Or else they find two-tone saddle shoes in thrift stores, or some kind of great thing to wear—not refugee shoes.

The trend away from black, all black, and only black has finally happened, after fifteen years of its being the only color you saw anywhere for any woman when you went out. Now the girls are wearing flamboyant beautiful old dresses, floral prints, paisleys, checks, plaids—even the Gap has those cute "sweetheart neckline" T-shirts in something other than black. They've got red, they've got rust, they've got turquoise—the white ones, in fact, have taken over, because they look so great on everyone. The guys have taken to wearing browns, greens, blues—only truly out-of-it types wear all black anymore, guys so cute they can get away with no style.

Tiffany has never taken a dance class in her life, but she used to work at the Palomino, the old-time country-western bar where Clint Eastwood movies took place when Sandra Locke wanted to be a CW singer. In those movies, for background you saw couples dancing together, this East Coast Swing stuff, so she learned there from whoever knew and would teach her—guys from the valley who remembered the fifties before the twist.

When Tiffany is about to teach the class, she begins by lining the girls up on one side, the guys on the other. Then, without a microphone or anything, dressed in her cutest outfits (at least I think they must be her cutest since they're so cute), and her short black hair and her nice tan skin, she begins showing the six-beat dance. Which is easy.

Before class we sat and spoke about her experiences and observations of the dance world.

"I used to be a manager at the Palomino; before that I was just the door girl, cashier there," she begins, easily. "I was more involved in the rockabilly and old country stuff. I used to go and see a lot of local bands; it was all country and rockabilly."

"So then you started teaching here."

"Over three years ago, my boyfriend got a gig here, so I started dancing when he was playing and they saw me dancing and invited to teach a class here. . . ."

"It's great," I say. "This class is the social event of the season. There's always such pandemonium. I love this place; I've been to Pasadena Ballroom Dance and their lindy classes sort of blend in with this."

"I'm more of a street dancer, and I've never taken any lessons. Everything I learned is from clubs, so I just took that all and incorporated it here. So it's more an East Coast Swing kind of thing, it's not so much lindy hop, though we do incorporate lindy hop moves in here."

"So how many people come here, seventy-five?"

"I get about sixty people in my dance lessons," she says, "and the Derby hires me to teach at parties. I did the Christmas party for Warner Brothers Records—I got dancers for that. And when we had a show at the Variety Arts Center, I had dancers for that as well. I've organized a lot of things, and I've just gotten a call for a USC student film. I'm going to get them dancers."

"I think they should have just a dance movie," I say. "It's just horrible when they have dancers and all they show are the reactions!"

She laughs. "Right."

"So how does your dance life fit into your day job? What do you do?"

"I'm into research and development for a fashion designer. I work for the owner of the division. This is like a moonlighting thing, the dance thing. It's fun and keeps me young."

Tiffany's boyfriend, PJ, not only has his own band, the Big Town 7, but he also plays in that swing orchestra that goes on the road, led by the ex-punker. I ask her about him.

"He's playing with Brian Seitzer, he's a keyboard player. They're doing really great, they've been on tour all summer long. Then when he's back in town, he's got his own band, Big Town Seven. They play the Orange County Blues Festival this weekend."

"It's so hard to think of Orange County with a blues festival," I say—the place is so Republican. "It's Orange County; they should have a Yellow Festival. Or Orange, but certainly not blue!"

Just then, one of her friends comes, Frank, and I ask them both about their style.

"What sort of shoes do you have; do you wear special shoes?"

"No," she replies, the only dancer who isn't concerned about shoes. "I just wear little flats. Little pointy fifties flats. The guys usually wear like Docs or wing tips."

"And don't they find that they stick?"

"My shoes are so old," Frank explains, "that they're slick on the bottom."

"Do you buy special clothes to dance in?"

"No, I just wear whatever I find in thrift stores, or whatever's around."

"It seems like everyone I know is in thrift stores, getting a look."

"It's a mixture—I think you've got your regular vintage people who dress head-to-toe vintage, and you've got people who are just getting into the scene, so they're wearing modern clothes, like regular khakis and stuff. And then you've got hipsters coming in, Hollywood hipsters . . ."

"Geriatric hipsters," I say.

"And then there are the people who work all day and come here. Those are the ones I admire the most—people who are too tired to do anything, and yet they *try*."

"What is this with the incredible old cars too?" I ask.

"Well, I have a fifty-one Chevy, but I'm selling it."

"Why, did you become an adult?" I ask.

"No, I just did a lot of work, I rebuilt the engine—I rebuilt everything to make it original. I did so much work on it that I finally just bought a regular car. Now, between my boyfriend's truck and my fifty-one Chevy and my car, it's hard moving all the cars around."

"So what did you get for a regular car?"

"A little station wagon."

"Ohhhhhhhhhh," I sighed. "I had a little station wagon. Nobody flirts with you anymore, no matter what, in a station wagon."

"It's great for thrift shopping, though!" she replies.

"Yeah," says Frank.

"It's more practical," we both agree.

Duke is a friend of Tiffany's who comes to stand next to me, and gives me his ideas of the scene. "I do swing, but I do rockabilly swing. Which is a little more radical than East Coast Swing."

"What's it like?"

"It's more physical, whereas this is easygoing. It's like flipping the girls. It's a lot closer to jitterbug than East Coast Swing."

"How come you got into *that*?"

"Into rockabilly? There's a lot of good rockabilly dance out there, it's a way to dance with women. . . ."

"You throw girls around?"

"I know." He laughs. "You know, it's the only time you get to throw a girl around, and not get arrested!" he jokes.

He says, "It's a lot like polka and swing at the same time."

I'm beginning to fall in love with Duke, he's so funny. He's so charming; he's so smart. Unfortunately, he's twenty years younger than me. If there is any way for sweet guys to meet, flirt, exchange amazing ideas, and flip girls around, this is it!

My experience with the Derby is everyone else's. That is, that the dance floor is too small and the band's so great, everyone is just dying to dance. What's a Hollywood newly learned East Coast Swing dancer to do?

After the last class that I saw Tiffany give, she and her regular partner, Scott, did a very fast and incredibly great dance to a piece of old-time rock and roll, like "Rock Around the Clock." You could see why everyone adores her; she's the funniest dancer in the world, with her three-inch high heels, her great outfits, and her angelic aura.

The great thing about East Coast Swing is that people who have never danced before can do it and have fun; people can get dressed up in their swank attire, they can wear two-tone shoes, smoke cigars, and be part of the Old Hollywood. At the same time, in some ways they can be a part of the very newest of Hollywood too, the part that wants to act, to participate in the scene, to be part of the action.

And unlike country, which is another great way to learn to dance, East Coast does not require surrendering punk values. You can be a totally cosmopolitan city person without cowboy boots and still dance like crazy.

In this country, where the music is so wonderfully entangled, you can dance to the blues in either country or swing. "Rock Around the Clock" can be a country song or a city song. Girls in circle skirts and bobby socks and flats can be from anywhere. Guys in jeans and T-shirts and Doc Martens can be country boys who have to drive tractors, or city boys who are "faux workers," just workers by dress.

You have to hand it to a dance that can take so many people in a beginner class from total ineptitude to somewhat getting it, through the land of pandemonium, and wind up with something so accomplished, clear, and in sync with those swing days of long ago, when all that kids wanted was to have fun and scare their elders.

East Coast Swing is an American triumph of engineering, a dance that can be learned and then done on the dance floor through only a brief stopover in the scary land of pandemonium when, for a brief moment you think, Maybe I can't do this, maybe I should have stayed home and watched TV, never gone out at all, and if I can't do this stupid step right, I'll just . . . — which is what everyone is thinking—when suddenly it clicks in, the pandemonium is no longer quite such a chaotic element. Suddenly you've got it, you've *done* it. And you know you can do it again, you do, you add a turn in fact, your face is no longer a big frown, you are smiling and so is your partner, the dark forest has been crossed, you are now home free, a modern person capable of East Coast Swing, ready to rock around the clock, should it be asked of you from that day forward. And it's been only forty-five minutes; for the next fifteen minutes of the class, you are ready for them to play some music, you are ready to really *dance*.

8

Sonny Watson, the Crest,
and West Coast Swing

West Coast Swing has the worst name in the world. It isn't seductive, it isn't wonderful, it doesn't *swing*, and it sounds like a stifled weird excuse for the name of a dance. And yet, the dance itself, like tango, is infinite and sexy. It should have a name like tango, a name like . . . I don't know what it should be called, but West Coast Swing sounds so Dance Class I and II. Whereas you cannot learn West Coast in a dance class, except maybe at Sonny's Watson's in the Crest, or maybe in Receda on Tuesday nights at 7:30 for Beginning West Coast Swing. West Coast Swing, in any version except the Crest, is wimp city.

When it first got going women called it the Sophisticated Lady of Swing. But maybe it should be called "Lady Swing" to keep that smoldering Billie Holiday kind of allure.

Sonny offers to meet me halfway between his house and mine (a West Coast Swing compromise). We decide Jerry's Deli will be good for our interview because he can sit outside, which is the only way anyone can smoke in L.A. anymore, in these terraces outside. Like Orlando, he smokes, but then anyone as great as he is can do whatever he wants, at least as far as I am concerned.

He arrives almost half an hour late, what he calls "California time" (which I always thought was only fifteen minutes late), but it's such a hot day, and he's the One, so . . .

With him he brings a huge heap of dance material, giving me a computer printout of the history of West Coast Swing, and along with this, his valuable history of dance, old magazines, the hoardings of a one-track mind, the tokens of an obsession for this one dance. If you didn't know what he did, you might think he was some computer nerd, pale from too much time indoors, slightly pudgy from no exercise and no desire to move at all. He is one of those men who could never get tan and should never have been brought up anywhere near the West Coast, much less be associated with its dance to such a degree. But here he is, the One.

Not that anyone in his classes, at least the men, will admit he's the One, because in West Coast everyone is such an anarchist. They all think nobody can teach them anything and they're only taking the class to learn a few steps. Period.

But then, West Coast Swing does not bring out the best in men; they suffer too much for too little glory. The women, in this dance, are the Ones.

Sitting down at the table outside (even though it was 108 degrees that day), the books and materials he's hauled in get laid down beside him, not to be shared or gotten pickle juice on, but to be viewed by me from a safe, teacher-to-student, respectful distance. Luckily I am used to weird men, having grown up with my father, who was always trying to convince the baroque musical community that they were playing Bach all wrong. This was not going to make him the most popular man in musicological circles, though some people believed him, because all he said was "Bach should be played on the instruments he composed for—the eighteenth-century violin, not violins invented to blast Beethoven all the way up to the rafters." People thought my father was the worst weirdo of all time.

So Sonny in his obsession is no weirdo to me, I mean, on a scale of one to ten, he's a seven and a half. Not that bad a weirdo at all, really. But then, the things that people in the valley get into their heads to be weird about are usually trucks, not *dancing!*

Looking at the photographs, I ask, "How long have you been dancing?"

"Seventeen years," he says.

"Is West Coast the same as Bob Willis? Do you know who he is?"

"Yeah, it's not the same.

"This book is by Arthur Murray; it's got a lot of good stuff, it's all about the history of dance mostly, goes back to the quadrilles, this is all swing."

"Can you get this from the library?"

"This is nineteen fifty; here's the *Life* magazine." He shows me one with swing dancers on the cover.

"Is this the famous edition of dancers the girls from Pasadena went to New York to find? The lindy hop?"

"I have that edition. This is Leon."

"So this is the famous edition that turned everybody on?" I wonder.

"Not turned everybody on. Swing's been going a lot longer than Tami and Erin Stevens."

"But teaching on the West Coast and all," I say.

"They helped find Frankie Manning," he says bleakly. "I've got tons of stuff."

"Tell me about your history." He hands me the history of West Coast Swing and agrees it's the general consensus of the dance's history. I say, "This is great. See, it just seems to me to have gotten great. I have been to the things given by Sandra Giles, and it seems to me the way you did it was just so . . ."

"Well, Sandra never did West Coast Swing, to be perfectly honest."

"What does she do?"

"Well, she's kind of an actress who got in with some of the dancers and decided to have these dances and fake her way along. I've known her for sixteen years and I'll tell you, every year she gets better and better—but she's not very good. Ten years ago, she was pathetic. She has a lot of fun, she loves it. It's part of her life. You don't have to be the greatest dancer to enjoy dancing, something a lot of people forget, especially with West Coast."

"Well, with East Coast you can always have a good time, even if it's your first day."

"Yes, correct."

"Even if it's your first fifteen minutes."

"I've got a whole list of movies; I can give you photocopies. . . ."

"Tell me your history," I said. "The story of your dance life!"

"I'm from California—the valley."

"I always thought this was a totally valley dance."

"It was basically born and bred here, in Hollywood. Back in the forties the lindy hop was very popular. As for the jitterbug, when it got into the fifties, a lot of the movies they were making had to do more with street dancing than the chorus line. It was going more toward Jerry Lewis and Dean Martin. They did a movie where they were in this ballroom, and they had these dancers dancing jitterbug. Anyhow, one of the things that helped form West Coast was that they didn't have wide-angle lenses, so they had to take the lindy hop, which was a circular dance, and start squeezing it into this little lens, and in the process the slot started to get more developed."

"I can't believe human beings would devise that slot."

"It wasn't really devised, it was an accident like I said because the movies had these lenses."

"But now there's the Hustle, I mean, people *willingly* put themselves in this slot."

"There are only two dances as far as I know that are slot dances and that's Hustle and West Coast Swing and that's California Hustle; New York Hustle is circular, it's quite a bit different."

"I'll never learn all these things. I came to dancing the most horrible way possible, through the tango."

"Oh, did you? Tango's a great dance. It's a passionate dance!"

"The trouble with it is, it drove me completely insane and I tried for years, but I had no balance."

"So anyhow, I was twenty-one and in the valley and a friend of mine was in the Marine Corps. I was going to college, but when I turned twenty-one I wasn't—"

"What were you taking in college?

"I was going to become a metallurgist. That's the science of metals."

"So West Coast fits right in with that."

"This friend of mine in the Marine Corps had gotten into dancing while he was there—he was into part disco and part Hustle. This was the seventies; I was born in nineteen fifty-nine. So he got out of the Marine Corps and he started telling me about dancing, which I didn't have a clue about, but I always wanted to dance."

"Don't you think everyone wants to dance?"

"No. The majority of people don't. Before becoming a teacher I used to think everybody wanted to, but as a teacher, no. A lot of people love to dance, probably over half the population would love to dance, but then there's a whole other group that doesn't even care to watch it.

"From there, he talked me into going to this country-and-western bar and when we walked in, they were doing swing. I always wanted to do swing as a kid; my parents did it."

"You had the genes!"

"When I was a kid I thought they were good dancers, now I think they stink. So he took me to this country bar—it was the Longhorn Saloon, just after *Urban Cowboy* came out—and I walked in and it was swing (I learned the two-step along the way, but actually, at the time, nobody had heard of West Coast Swing). So I started out with country swing at first and from there found out about East Coast Swing and learned that. Then I heard about this thing, it was actually called Western Swing and Eastern Swing at that time . . . I heard about this Western Swing, and I'd never even seen it so I paid no attention to it.

"So I started competing in swing competitions in which the majority of the people did East Coast and a couple came in and did West Coast. That's the first time I saw it and they got first place; obviously they were very good. I talked to them about where to learn to do it and stuff, and they didn't really have a clue. One was Charlotte Janson; she still dances today."

"Was she wearing high heels?"

"Yeah. From there I started checking around. A place called the Learning Tree University had a couple that did West Coast Swing, and they gave lessons. My girlfriend at the time talked me into going over there, and we went over there, and they were the worst lessons in the world."

"It's hard to teach West Coast Swing—to teach beginning it's very hard."

"Very hard, beginning especially. It assumes you have a basic dance background at the start. A lot of people start with nothing. But it assumes you have a basic dance background, any kind of dance background, but West Coast Swing is the dancers' dance. East Coast would be more for the beginner; West Coast is more for the East Coaster who's gotten bored and wants to move on. It assumes that you have some kind of background, have some rhythm and some timing. And if you don't, you have to acquire it at the same time as learning West Coast, which is the hard part.

"From there I went to Phil Adams in Long Beach. He's very good. From the West Coast class that I had started at the Learning Tree I heard that Phil Adams was going to be out in the valley teaching an eight-week class. They said I should check it out, it was pretty much what I was looking for, and from there it was just learning, learning, learning, every place I could, from anybody I could."

"And so how long have you been teaching?"

"I started teaching in nineteen eighty-three."

"You started teaching at the Crest?"

"No, just about every nightclub there is out here, out in the valley. By now I'm older, now I don't want to be seven nights a week teaching in a nightclub. But at one time I was teaching seven nights a week in different nightclubs. And a lot of studios—I've worked for different studios throughout the valley—some of them I've gone in and helped their teachers learn West Coast so they could teach it."

"I met someone who took a lot of lessons at one of these places and he was mad because when he came to you, he couldn't do anything."

"Well, some of the places, they're more a social place with dance thrown in. As far as the dancing part of it goes, a lot of what they teach is not in the ballpark of the rest of the world. But, well, there's a thing called country western, I don't know if you know too much about that, it's all over, the two-step. When the teacher doesn't know what the hell they're doing and teaches it totally awkward-looking, the excuse is 'Well, it's country. It's supposed to look that way, it's supposed to look shitty, it's supposed to look back of the barn, horsing around type stuff.' And that's just not true. And a lot of people, when they teach bad ballroom, they call it 'American.'

"But still, some of those places turn out bad dancers that can't dance with the rest of the world. They make everyone have a good time, they teach them to lead and follow, and that's all they intend to do. And then places that teach East Coast, they don't like West Coast.

"There are two families, the East Coast and the West Coast, and they both hate each other. They shouldn't, but unfortunately, some of the teachers create that wall. And so if someone's interested in West Coast and you teach them and it's bitchin' and they like it, they're more likely to go with West Coast. If they don't like it, they're more likely to stay with East Coast."

"Well, maybe their students aren't good enough to do West Coast."

"Anybody's good enough—it's always the teacher, never the student. I've taught bad students as well as good ones. Some of it, obviously, if they don't show up for lessons, there's nothing much you can do, but . . ."

"How much are private lessons?"

"I charge forty-five dollars."

"Well, I'm lucky because I'm a writer so my ego doesn't depend on being a great dancer and basically I'm just trying to get the feeling of the dances and to try not to look too horrible."

"You have to do the best you can," he said.

"It seems to me if there's not a really strong, a mystical presence, like Orlando the tango teacher, when he's gone everybody's at each other's throats."

"It's sort of comical," he says. "People tend to argue, they get different ideas. I used to teach at a club when the play *Tango Argentino* came to town. When the play came out it opened up a whole new audience for this tango; it was great enough to start all the tango there is today. At one of the clubs where I was teaching my two-hour class, I'd have Orlando come down and teach an hour tango class with Miranda."

"I would have loved to see them dance. By the time I met Orlando, he was so mad at Miranda he wouldn't dance with her anymore."

"They were good. I don't think Orlando's the best tango dancer I've seen, but he's the most consistent out here of the better tango dancers."

"He's the nicest."

"Has his English gotten any better?"

"No, he's too old a dog to learn new tricks. He knows words like 'shoelace.' "

"Tango kind of comes and goes out here. Right now they've got the play *Forever Tango*."

"Well, I loved *Tango Argentino* because the people were older and they looked like they knew their partners and they made you feel alive. Usually when you see dancers, they're all twenty years old and interchangeable. Most of the people I know. I think tango is kind of like West Coast Swing in a weird kind of a way, because the leads are extremely occult."

"They're very related in a lot of ways, as far as a dancer's dance, the equivalent of tango—American tango and Argentine tango. It would be much easier to learn American tango first and then learn Argentine. American, you can take one lesson at it and have a good time with it. East Coast Swing would be American tango, West Coast Swing would be Argentine."

"West Coast swing is sort of adult, thoughtful, slow."

"You have to think," he says.

"You can do it to the blues," I add.

"You can do it to anything," he said, "even tango music. Anything that's four-four time, and tango is four-four time."

"Did you try tango, did you like it?"

"I liked it, but I didn't like it as much as West Coast."

"Well, West Coast to me looks like a sexy James Bond kind of dance."

"Yeah."

"Like a sophisticated, you know . . ."

"Well, at one time it was called Sophisticated Swing."

"When I was growing up in L.A. in the fifties, at our school they did a dance called the Choke, a pachuco dance like Pony Swing."

"A lot of the research I've done—in my experience, dancers in Northridge could be totally doing a different dance than they're doing in Studio City. And they can be doing the same dance and calling it a different name."

"In L.A. everything is so far away, though." I sigh.

"I generally live in Studio City. I grew up in Granada Hills, I like it here."

"Do you fall in love with good dancers or just anybody?"

"Anybody."

"You mean, you'd fall in love with just anybody?"

"Well, they've got to have requirements. Good-looking for one, personality is probably the second thing, maybe the first, but in my thing I don't think I'm attracted to them if they're not good-looking to begin with. Dancing is not even an issue, whether they dance or not, 'cause I can teach them to dance. If they don't want to dance, it's fine, I can go out dancing myself. For a woman, on the other hand, I think it would be a different thing."

"Have you ever met anyone you couldn't teach to dance? Do

you think there's such at thing as being atonal, of not having any rhythm?"

"But usually, as far as not being able to teach someone to dance, it's because they don't practice, they don't listen, they have an ego, they know it all already, they overanalyze everything . . ."

"That's me."

"Well, like they say, Why do you want me to do this? What benefit is it to you that I do this? People are really weird. So instead of teaching, you get into defending why they should do it—and you feel like an idiot doing it, like, Why am I defending this step?"

"What do you do now that you're not teaching in clubs?"

"I teach every day, privates and group classes in the studio. B and B Dance Center, it's in Van Nuys, Burbank and Woodman Blvd."

"So do you still like Phil Adams?"

"I have more respect for Phil than any other pro I know."

"I love the two-step because it's fun."

"It is fun."

"Did you ever do any salsa and that kind of stuff?"

"I've been to the Mayan and I've been to the Sportsman's Lodge. I don't go out dancing near as much, but I still enjoy it. No place in particular. The Press Box is small and crowded, it's a lot of fun, and it's got some of the best dancers in the southern California area. The Crest is about four times the size of the Press Box; it's probably the next highest to the Press Box for swing."

"People who dance every single day of their life."

"They've got a lot of energy, the energy makes them find the time. Some people, like lawyers and musicians and firemen, they work very hard and they do their job, but they're out dancing seven nights a week. And I know people who've got no job and that's all they do. Go dancing."

"What do you think a West Coast Swing romance would be like? Do people ever fall in love with each other in the dance classes?"

"Yes, a lot of people get together in the dance class, and a lot of people get broken up 'cause of dancing. What I've seen over the years is if a couple has a good relationship, dancing will enhance it. If they've got a bad relationship, dancing will wreck it. But again, in a social situation people with a bad relationship will tend to get more jealous and more insecure with their own dancing and not be as sociable, argue when someone is being sociable, stuff like that. The people who've got a good relationship . . ."

"West Coast Swing is such a sexy dance, you don't want your lover to do too well with someone else."

"I don't think it has to do with the dance; it has to do with the boundary on the relationship. If I was golfing and I was very good at golfing, and my significant other went out golfing with Joe Blow and he was a better golfer than I was, I think it would leave me a little insecure there too. The impression factor would scare me, but if it was a good relationship, the impression factor I don't think would do that."

"I think a lot of people, they're miserable on the floor."

"Well, they're miserable before they started dancing. They came to dancing to try and find something. There's one thing that our society lacks out here; it's social graces. They don't know how to socially interact, they don't know how to—they know how to *fight* with each other, but they don't know how to socially get along with each other and dancing over a couple of years really teaches you a lot of social skills. People with bad social skills tend to look at dancing and think, Well, this might help. They get in there, and they don't realize they just have such a bad attitude."

"I think some people were just raised by wolves."

"People think because of how they dance, they've got a right to be however they want. Being one of the leaders of the swing community, I can tell you there are some people who come in and disrupt the organization. They come in and argue that they don't want to pay the cover charge; they use their 'irate skills' to get in for free. So basically, the bottom line is that I say no and they get pissed off and leave. There are people who come in, take a private lesson with you, and they think everything else should be free, so they argue. Then there are the people who come in, pay the cover charge every week, and they think they deserve a free private for doing it. There are always people who like to finagle ways of getting things for free. They'll get into a knock-down-drag-out about it. At that point, you have to say, 'It's time for you to leave.'

"Then there's the flip side of the coin, people who will basically do anything to help out the dancing. The part that kills me is that the dancers who dance so well, they won't even talk to people who are new and can't dance that well. To understand that way of thinking, you need to realize that when you go out to dance, you want to have a good time. Dance structure is built like a pyramid and obviously all the poor dancers are at the bottom, all the skilled are at the top. It's a very small group at the top, very large at the bottom. Let's say your average nightclub dancer is about a quarter of the way up from the bottom, and everybody thinks they're great. So they usually start to get a little bit of an attitude.

"But when you get about halfway up the pyramid, a lot of those dancers have been doing it a long time—they've been answering questions like you wouldn't believe. They've gone out dancing, they've paid their six bucks to get in, and they've got this one lady hogging their time all night long. Show me this, show me that, help me with this . . . and the dancer does not have a good time—why should they? They had to work through it, they got there, they know how to do it, and there are people looking for a free ride.

"There are people who come in who are generally attuned to learning and try to make sure everybody has a good time. They dance with the good as well as the bad dancers, but good dancers—everybody wants to dance with a good dancer. And when you walk into a nightclub, they're only going to play a hundred fifty songs at most a night. But you can't dance a hundred fifty dances straight, who would want to? To begin with, you don't like every song. Really, you look at any club, they are not the best dancers, most are just social dancers going for fun. Whereas the top dancers . . .

"Part of being a good dancer too is that it's enjoyable having people want to dance with you, just knowing that they do. You walk in and you just know it, you don't think about it—there's that allure that comes in with you, no matter how much you dance with the beginners, there always are some who feel you ignored them."

"In ballroom dancing, they won't dance with you unless you spend a fortune on private lessons," I insert.

"Well, as a teacher everyone wants to be your friend and it's tough because a lot of the people you tend to start to like. I can't tell you how many students I was really feeling a closeness to, but once the lessons were over, we were no longer friends; they've moved to another teacher. Teachers have feelings, too, and you miss people after a while. When people leave it's kind of sad. You go out of your way for some people because you do feel you're friends with them and then over the years you realize that that's how some people work; they get more from you if they're your friend. So you tend not to try to get as close. And I'm not talking physically close, although some teachers do that. I'm talking about when you like their personality and they act like your friends, but the friendships are based on what two people need from each other. A lot of time it's a false friendship, and teachers after a while start to back away from it.

"There's a whole life to being a dancer, a whole different life being a dance instructor, a whole different life being a competitor. You have to be a lot more responsible if you're a dance instructor. Being a top dance instructor means that you're all that—you are the top competitor, you are the top teacher, you are the top social person, you are the top popular person. Even though there are people who are just about equal out there, you are the top and you get to experience all those lives, whereas some people only get to experience a section of it. And some people experience just the teacher part of it.

"Some people aren't that great as a dancer or a competitor, but they are good as a teacher for beginners because they spend a lot of time on it, even though that teacher is only going to be around for six months to a year."

"We had some teachers at In Cahoots teaching beginners, but they had no idea what a beginner was," I said. "No idea."

"Well, a lot of teachers have never been beginners themselves. I know it sounds funny, but they jumped into the intermediate class and stayed there for five years and finally got it. Now they're teachers."

"Well, I like being a beginner because I like to start from scratch."

"Well, the beginners, there's a lot of innocence—just like a child—they can laugh and look stupid and not pay attention to people. Being a beginner was probably the best time in my whole dance life. Everything was new, everything was an adventure, everybody was new, and every song was new. Just today I've danced to 'In the Mood' five zillion times. Things change, you know."

"But not with the same partner," I point out.

"That's one thing that changes."

"In West Coast Swing it seems to me you have to bend your body in ways it's not going to be bent unless you are a belly dancer."

"If you want to dance that way," he said. "See, West Coast can be whatever you want it to be. It can be sexy, it can be nonsexy, it can be fun, it can be serious, it can be a lot of straight lines, it can be a lot of bent lines. It can be a lot of body movement, it can be no body movement, it can be a lot of footwork, it can be no footwork, it can be lots of spins, it can be no spins. It's whatever you want to do. West Coast Swing is strictly a personality dance, between your personality and the music's personality; it's whatever you put together. It's like tango; you learn the steps, but you've got to interpret the music. In the beginning you're not interpreting the music, you're trying to learn the steps, you're trying to twist your body and do things with your legs that people just don't do, so in the beginning it can be difficult."

"I love the look of West Coast Swing, it's like a Frank Sinatra song."

"It can be whatever you want it to be. You don't have to be the best dancer of anything, speaking from my experience of teaching a whole hell of a lot of people, running dances, and everything else. If you have a nice personality, that's all you need if you just have a desire to dance. If you have a shitty personality, you better be a good dancer, because otherwise it ain't going to happen. You don't have to be the sexiest person on the floor, you just have to be a nice person."

"And know how to talk the language. If someone says do this, you have to do everything."

"It's a workout."

This time, after our interview, when I go to the Crest for the third time, I take the beginning West Coast class once more. Finally I discover I am able to do two Sugar Pushes, the easier kind and the kind that makes the girl look like a languid snake—a look that for me personifies West Coast and is, right now, all I've ever wanted out of life.

If there's one thing about this dance, it's the way it makes women look like languid snakes in certain moves, and really, this is the first time I've come anywhere near the Look, which is all I wanted. I feel like a very sophisticated lady at the Crest in Receda, in spite of being in the valley.

The first time I saw West Coast Swing, I thought there was nothing to it. The woman just looked like she was dancing around by herself with the man kind of hanging in there. Occasionally the man was doing something but only just on the edges. Then I realized, that's the dance.

In Receda, where Cindy Williams is from, they have odd luxuries like the Crest. The Crest is the ugliest dance club in the whole world, but has a floor four sizes as big as those of most other clubs. The first time I came it seemed their parking lot in front hardly had enough space. When I asked the woman who takes the money where to park, she said, "We have *five* parking lots, they're free, all down that street."

So it's ugly, but it has five parking lots and a huge dance floor. You can get used to a place with five free parking lots and a nice big dance floor, just out of convenience.

Anyway, at the Crest, Sonny Watson teaches a four-week beginner class in which he expects students to start out in the first week learning the most basic steps and move on to Whips and Sugar Pushes by the last Tuesday of the month. A person paying $6 a session, who wanted to, could learn West Coast Swing by increments, little by little getting the idea of how on earth Sonny's partner, Kris Haggarty, looks so incredibly gorgeous doing this one particular thing.

Fortunately, the lighting at the Crest is so low that even if you could see yourself in the mirrors, which are waist high, you can't see yourself really. For me, to learn a dance in a room with no mirrors is a lot less nerve-racking. It's just hell to realize that we look so befuddled and inept, when our gorgeous teacher is such a snake vampire of beauty.

In popular culture the valley has held on to such amazing things as the Car Culture. For a while they used to sashay down Van Nuys Boulevard on certain nights, the pickups with all the lights on top, the cars altered or painted with flames in front. And along with that culture, still flourishing in the valley, are the swing dancers, who Robert Irwin, the conceptual artist, used to join when he was a teenager in the forties, going to such clubs as the Jungle Club in Inglewood on Monday, the Dollhouse in the valley on Tuesday, and so on.

Irwin said in an interview, "When you got it going real smooth, you could literally get to the point where you were almost floating off the ground, acting as counterweights for each other. It was absolutely like flying, just a natural high."

I wonder if that dance he did so smoothly that he felt like flying was a version of West Coast Swing, since when you see really good West Coast dancers, they do seem like they're flying, and the counterweight thing *is* the dance.

I decided the next step was to find out more about the other half of the duo, Sonny's partner, Kris Haggarty. I asked her, "How did you get into this?"

"I've known Sonny for years, I had taken a class of his years ago, probably about eight years ago. Then one night at a club, a country-western bar, he came in and I asked if he still gave private lessons and we became partners."

"Have you done contests?"

"Oh, yeah, I loved it—I love West Coast Swing a lot. One thing a lot of people find when they get into West Coast Swing is that it's an unlimited dance. You can't possibly get bored from it because there is so much you can do in West Coast Swing, plus you can go anywhere and do it in any club. There's always music you can do West Coast Swing to. It's not like the two-step or salsa or Latin, where you have to have a certain song or tempo."

"Right, and you can do it to the blues; the blues are so great," I say. (I mean, to me, the blues are *our* tango, but West Coast is the only dance you can do to it.)

"You can pretty much do West Coast to anything. I've done it to a tango, I've done it to a cha-cha also."

"Do you make up your own costumes and all that?"

"We do, I do. The contests are all over the United States, but the main one is in Anaheim. It's called the U.S. Open, and it's held on Thanksgiving weekend. I've been in it the past six years."

"Have you ever won it?"

"I've won—actually I got second place in the Advanced Jack and Jill there. We've also gotten fifth. That's the granddaddy of all the contests, that's what everybody aims for."

"Is there something called the master class?"

"Fifty-five and over is the masters' division, they usually hit the showcase of the main contest division."

"West Coast Swing," Kris says, "is a hard dance for the woman to learn at first. It takes, I would say, about a year to get good at it, but that's a year out of your life compared to a whole lifetime of fun."

"It seems that with these partner dances, the older you get the better you are!" I agree.

"Oh, yeah, when your mentality changes! When you're young, you look at partner dancing as being an old-fogey dance, you know. But when you get older, you think, Well, this could be cool."

"Oh," I said, "but *you're* not old!"

"*Thank* you."

"Is your boyfriend a dancer too?"

"Actually, no. He wants to learn how to dance just so he can dance with me, but that's about it. He works at the commissary at Warner Brothers and right now he's trying to direct also, finish his first film project."

"The reason I ask is that I am also trying to write a romance here—Sonny says people often break up in this scene."

"Like I said," Kris said, "it's a soap opera here. You look around, people get together, but then they're breaking up and going out with two people on the side"—she indicates people in the next booth—"you know, it's a soap opera."

The only trouble with West Coast, in fact, according to other dancers, is that once someone learns this dance, they insist on doing it to all other music. They do it to two-step, they do it to everything. For them the idea that any other dances exist gets lost in the sexy shuffle of West Coast Swing. There is torque and release, this elegant smoothness, the surprise of it all and how wonderful it is.

There's nothing like a Jack and Jill, according to my friend Paul McClure, the two-step teacher. It is the time when, in a contest, someone points to you and you dance with someone you've never seen before or danced with before. Paul says there is nothing more thrilling than watching two people dance together for the first time and adapt each other's moves, limitations, and so on to their own moves and limitations. To win an Advanced Jack and Jill as Kris Haggarty has, at the Anaheim contest, must really be something to see.

At some of these places, they have exhibition dancing, which is a lot like the partner skating at the Olympics—three or four minutes of excruciating moves that leave the partners soaking and exhausted. But usually in West Coast nobody ever gets soaking or exhausted because it is the ultimate dance for dancing all night long without sweat. It's a dance to keep women changing like a kaleidoscope, but never is it too fast. Never is the woman *compelled* to get a move on, like with salsa.

The more I saw West Coast Swing, the less I liked salsa. But then, if salsa is a Latin thing, then maybe I'm just too much of a Cajun-Jewish mouse for it. The way Latin dancing has been taken up by the "kids," they want to dance only if the music is the loudest, the fastest, and the most intense. The dances of long ago like slow cha-chas are regarded with contempt. The "kids" will abandon a band that plays slow songs; they don't want to be associated with the "old" dancers, even sincere old dancers who dance great.

In West Coast Swing, anyone who does this dance well is regarded with amazement and awe. The premise that music has to be loud and fast is the opposite of West Coast Swing, where the music has to be slow and audible. This is a dance for women. It is a dance of women's moves; for the men to learn their part, they must learn "less, don't do anything."

Men have to learn to take whatever the woman's going to do and then help her do it. In Sonny's beginning class, he tries to explain this to the men in the class, that they don't lead necessarily, so much as help the women do the dance they want to do.

But the men can't take a woman who doesn't know this dance and help her fake it through; if you don't know the dance, you don't know this dance.

With salsa and East Coast and the cha-cha even, if you've had a lesson or two, you can pass. Or if you're the lady, you can be led by someone like my friend Maurice and look good.

But to look good in West Coast at the Crest on a Tuesday night, learning the first style, steps, and rhythm is *hard*. And as you get more able to do this dance, then the next thing that's required of you is to dance to the music, taking into account every sad note, every trumpet, every accident of beat.

What's most interesting about this dance is that the lady has a choice as to what she's going to do at least some of the time. Dancing in a slot, six feet long or so, back and forth, as this and the L.A. Hustle both do, is amazing—the incredible amount of nuance, slitheryness, and beauty all this can be. Plus, you can do it to the blues and to "Fever," my favorite song. You can even do it to Ray Charles.

Anyway, I will try to learn this dance, commit for a year. Maybe it will be possible.

The Finale and L.A. Now

When I first began this book, what I wanted to show about people who went dancing was that, in spite of everything, this was a way to have fun and not only was it fun to dance, but you could lose weight like there was no tomorrow. I saw a lot of people come in at first looking so-so, but soon they were trim and healthy or at least having fun trying to get that way. One thing is true about dancing, or even entering one beginner's dance class—it makes most people suddenly realize that if they want to look cute, there's a way to get there without suffering by dieting or exercising in a gym.

Because at the gym, though you might like to, you can't really flirt your head off, whereas with partner dancing, looking at the person whose arms you are in, or who is in your arms, is part of the dance. Smiling, too, is part of it all, but mainly when you do social dancing, except for something just too silly like the polka. The whole dance should be, if you're following Renée's belief in the least, a flirtation.

Most people get flirting drummed out of them nowadays, what with everything being so politically correct and such a bummer. So to be able to do something that is flirting but is also something else—being one with the music—well, this is a great thing. It's like making art with someone you've never met and might never meet again, but only on the dance floor and only for that one dance.

Then again, there is a lot that can go wrong if you enter this dance world as a couple, trying to take a beginner's class. One or the other of you might soon want to move on to not-such-beginner stuff while the other is still stuck, unable to grasp the basics, feeling like they never will.

Jim Hines, my old friend who knows a lot, told me that in his opinion, eighty percent of women can and love to dance, whereas only twenty percent of men do. So right there we've got trouble. In fact, most men don't want to get anywhere near dancing because, let's face it, it's not staying home watching the Super Bowl, is it? It involves getting up off the couch and into a car and paying money, and unless it's the East Coast Swing beginner's class, which is the only dance, really, that men can do after only one lesson in Tiffany's class, most men will think, 'This is just ridiculous, forget it.' But then, Tiffany had the kind of temperament where even if you interrupted her on a dance floor, she'd gladly stop everything and explain, whereas most teachers, if they never have to see a beginner anywhere but in their class, it's too soon.

Paul McClure, too, could bear to show people who couldn't dance how to do it in his beginner's class, letting new people hang around after and ask him questions. He gladly showed them what to do and explained things carefully and politely, but then he's just a saint in my opinion. You have to be in country or you're not country.

So it's no wonder that men who try other kinds of dancing soon realize they're never going to be as good as their wife or girlfriend. They just hate the whole thing, unless they're driven there, like some guys to salsa, because the music is so great. They just love it and manage to hang in long enough in Salsa One to pass as not that bad after all.

In tango, of course, the men who come have usually been exposed to other dances. If they were able to do regular ballroom, they might not think it so bad in spite of how bad it actually is, especially if they have a wife or girlfriend who's bound and determined that's what they're going to do. But by the time men get to tango, they pretty much know how to learn dances. They do not, as I so stupidly did, attempt tango just from scratch when what I should have done was gone to regular ballroom dancing and learned at least what it means to follow, i.e., don't move until the man moves and that's that.

There are some men going to the Cajun dances who simply love to dance, and somehow know how. They can waltz at least somewhat and manage to catch on to the Cajun jitterbug after a very short time, even the fancy turns and arm work that girls love so much in a partner.

And there are even some men who come across West Coast Swing and decide it's not that hard. They might even master it, though what is in it for them I don't know—they do all the work. They have to react perfectly to whatever the girl decides to do, and if they don't, they get hard looks and nasty remarks like "You're on the six, I'm on the eight, what are you, stupid or something?"

Partner dancing when it's done well is euphoria, floating through time and space and music with people having just so much fun, and it's really so great, it breaks my heart so many men find it sissy stuff, but they do.

That's men for you.

Most men, even Maurice, will come to a club, stand there looking around and listening to the music, and if you ask them to dance, they say, "Not now, maybe later. I don't like this band."

I wanted to end it that if you went dancing, your troubles would wash away and sorrow could never hurt you—nothing, in fact, could.

I believed that no matter what had befallen me in the time I wrote the book—things that seemed much too horrible at the time, stuff like my mother breaking her hip, the house filled with contractors, the plumbing driving me crazy—no matter how boring and tiresome these things were, all I had to do was go dancing. Then I would be euphoric and as one with the music, doing a simple dance like a waltz, and feeling like nothing could stop me.

Wrong, as usual.

I was going to end my book on a note of triumph, having finally learned how to follow. I think it was Renée who broke my terrible habit of beginning when I thought we were supposed to start rather than letting the man begin and then turning to a sort of mushlike thing that could be led to do anything. Anyway, I had finally managed to break the code; go anywhere, dance with anyone, do any dance that was currently popular with a partner. Even though I was never going to do West Coast Swing (what with this knee I had that kept hurting, shooting pain, every time I attempted to do that dance), I could still appreciate those who did it well; it just made my mouth water.

I thought once the book came out I'd be dancing not just every night, but everywhere. That Paris, for example, would welcome me with open arms (I know they do tango there). That Japan, whose royal family once imported Orlando they were so crazy about his tango, well, they'd just help with my worldwide chain. It would be better than Arthur Murray, because we wouldn't just have ballroom, we'd have everything, salsa, samba, the works. I later heard from my friend Roger Webster, who recently went there, that even China has these public squares where people dance ballroom. Slaves or not, the people have some fun anyway.

My dance chain would be better than anything, and if only it began in Los Angeles in some gorgeous old place, maybe the

Green Hotel in Pasadena, well, I'd be jolly well set for life. At least I'd never get fat; I'd be dancing too much.

Well, wrong again, as usual.

Since I first sent these pages in, many things have happened to me that would throw a person who didn't have dancing to look forward to into a slough of despond. I unfortunately got half burned up after a Sunday brunch in Pasadena, sitting in my car, trying to light a cigar. Okay, the car was a '68 VW bug, but still, you don't expect your skirt to go up in flames just from trying to light a cigar after behaving so well at brunch that you felt you deserved a cigar.

I had third-degree burns over fifty percent of my body. But still I drove home, being sure that all I needed was aloe from my own aloe plant, which I had been saving for just such an emergency. I thought, "I'll put aloe on it and maybe not tonight but tomorrow, I'll be out dancing."

Wrong, wrong, wrong.

Well, that was the end of my dance happy ending. I wound up in the ICU for six weeks, in rehab hospitals for another two months. Arriving in the hospital, I felt that I at least had a chance, because if you're going to survive being in "guarded" condition, you have to have several things going for you. One, you should be in otherwise okay condition, which I was; and two, you should have something above and beyond everyday life to look forward to. I did—I wanted once more to do that Cajun waltz.

It's amazing. There I was, a puddle basically, but in my head I was out in South Pasadena, at the War Memorial Hall (across the street from the restaurant where my accident happened), dancing with maybe this one guy I met there, a Cal Tech kid named John, the best waltzer in Western civilization. In my head, when they told me if I lived I might not be able to walk, and even then undergoing physical therapy would be just the worst, I thought nothing they could do to me would be worse than not being in the dance world. Let the torture begin!

First, I had to learn to walk again. Going downstairs was a completely scary thing; at first I even had to use a walker, like some old Walter Matthau guy, dragging myself up and down the corridors, trying to get my strength back. I was in so much pain that the nurses couldn't believe me when I told them, "You know, I used to be charming before I got here."

They told my sister in the hospital, "This is the worst thing that human beings can ever go through; do you think she can make it?"

"Make it?" she said. "What do you mean?"

I told them I was a dancer, so I was not the usual fifty-year-old because at least, before this, I had been strong and in shape.

Well, my poor sister didn't know what to do but pray, but I more or less thought that I might survive if I followed their lead and did everything they told me. I was not going to just lie there like a puddle, succumbing to terror and whatever it is that kills people, psychologically, when they get things like this. I might not know much, but I had at least learned to follow. Not that I didn't complain, of course.

Once I entered the ICU, I was allowed only five visitors, even though I had lots of friends and some were mad they couldn't come see me. Only Maurice, out of the entire dance world, actually sent me cards (almost every day) and kept up personally. In the dance world, unless you're out there, they think you have "squared up" on them (as Lord Buckley used to say). You get married or something respectable and won't be back till whoever you decided was so great never wants to see you again, or the impulse to dance just overtakes you one night, and you have to see what's happening in tango again. A lot of women I met, in fact, had one real life at home with a man they loved, and a dance life with men they just loved for dancing, but didn't see otherwise. On the dance floor, in fact, these women could be extremely sexy and seductive and seem totally abandoned, but off the floor they were as ladylike as could be. The only proposition they remotely wanted to hear was "Do you want to dance this cha-cha or what?"

Of course, men who were really great dancers didn't have to have a real life at home, because dancing was their real life. They could find women rich enough to support them. If the women suddenly got uppity and began demanding the man dance only with them, the guy could easily move on to someone less boring but just as rich.

"We're all looking for Mr. Singer," Jim Hines once explained. We were sitting outside in his car, waiting for Orlando, who was his usual late self. There were always tons of people for Orlando's classes, so he was never on time, but if you took a private lesson he was exactly on time and so were you.

"Mr. Singer?" I said. "Who's that?"

"Mr. Singer?" Jim said, "He was Isadora Duncan's husband, you know, in the movie? The guy who invented Singer sewing machines and was so rich, remember, he lived in a mansion?"

"Right," I said. "Poor guy, he married her, but she was such a dancer, she just took off and went to Russia."

"Mr. Singer is who we want, someone who's so rich he marries a dancer and doesn't really mind. He was just glad to help out."

I thought, is that was all the dancers want—Mr. Singer? Well, it might be true. If you marry someone rich enough, you'll never have to worry, you can have dances anywhere you want. You could open the Atlas every night and it wouldn't matter if it didn't make money on dancers; you'd just have it there anyway, for your own amusement. But the funny thing was, I knew people rich enough to have kept the Atlas from losing Johnny Crawford's band when they could no longer afford him. They could even have put in a portable dance floor made of wood (like the one Robert Duvall supposedly took with him on location so he could dance tango wherever he was). But even this woman who seemed to have untold wealth, and who loved the Atlas and was sad when the place no longer had Johnny, never deemed it her place to take things into her own hands and keep those Thursday nights afloat. Perhaps she just preferred thinking of herself as a victim of circumstance like the rest of us, rather than the Mr. Singer who might have, on Isadora's urging, seen to it that it didn't go under.

Of course, Mr. Singer was a man, so he was used to having to shell out dough. Rich heiresses, who were married for their looks in the first place, think it's still their looks that ought to be a prize above rubies. It's not their job, no matter how old they have since become, to keep anything going just because they can afford to do it.

But of course, if you're rich enough—like Judith Krantz—you can go to the Beverly Wilshire Hotel every weekend, dance ballroom with your husband, and never mind that no one else can afford it. In fact, you probably prefer a place that you can always go to where it's not too jammed. Where you can, if you like, dance the night away to a great band that's not as perfect as Johnny Crawford's, but is good enough for the rich to look forward to, at least.

The truth about a Mr. Singer is that it has to be a man who can afford things, not a woman. Because women, in the dance world, expect to be treated as though they are as young as they still think they are, despite all the face-lifts and elective "help."

(Me, I think I've had all the plastic surgery I'll ever want just from these unelective skin grafts.)

Believe me, if I were rich I'd have kept the Atlas scene alive, just out of sheer civic pride, so something in Los Angeles would be wonderful enough to go on. But then, I'm a woman who isn't rich so I know what it is to lose something great and be unable to keep it afloat, no matter how many people I drag there to see the show.

L.A. Now

When I was so rudely swept away, most of the people probably thought, "Well, there goes another person, saying they're doing one thing—writing a book—and then vanishing from the face of the earth." But now I'm back, more or less.

So, because I was out of commission for so long, everything I wrote has changed, and probably will again, dance scenes being the rudely yanked-up-by-the-roots things they are. In tango, the Mark Celaya and Joan Yarfitz event was doing rather well while I was gone. They have now expanded their Friday-night tango class from 7:00 to 8:30 and their dance afterward is now so packed that there are over a hundred people coming—and this costs $10. A lot of them are the younger crowd from Cal Tech (the same kind who make it to In Cahoots, the adorable scientists), and it's great to be turning on the kids, keeping the dance alive. It's in Burbank, on 2006 West Magnolia, upstairs in a place called the Burbank Realtor Hall. Today Mark is so busy. He actually produced the show last year at the Hollywood Bowl, or at least the dancers, and 51,000 people attended over a three-day weekend. If you look for "tango music" on the Web, you'll eventually come to him because he distributes tango music. He says he has gotten 31,000 hits on his Web site, so if you can figure out the Internet, be my guest. If you can't, you'll just have to go to Burbank, which, God knows, is easier, but then, I'm here.

"The kids from Cal Tech are really amazing; they're a lot more mature than most of the older people. They have better manners and they learn quickly; they're great," Mark told me. "You know, they don't study tango for three months and turn into critics." Mark also arranges exhibitions and knows all the world-class tango dancers. He was able to get them for the Hollywood Bowl events, which was why, apparently, they turned out to be such a hit.

At Pasadena Ballroom Dance, the lindy hop bug has so taken sway that it's all they can have for the Saturday-night dances. I went there recently (with Maurice) and it began at 7:00 or so with a jitterbug class, only there were three hundred kids there and some really young. They serve only lemonade and popcorn and it's in a church, so kids can go and not be in trouble.

They had a band, but it only played fast and faster, and the kids with all that energy didn't care that for four solid hours, it seemed like, all they'd do was fast and faster; they liked it. There are the kids who dress in old clothes, rifling through thrift stores for exactly the right thing.

Of course, if they're like the ones before, they all buy their shoes at this place also on Magnolia (the same street where Mark's tango thing is), because Burbank is Glendale now, totally dance demented.

But then, even in Beverly Hills, they've now started Friday and Saturday nights at the Beverly Hilton, in the Coconut Club (named in honor of the old Coconut Grove). You pay $20 and can dance to great swing bands, and my wonderful friend Doz, whom I met originally at the Atlas and who loved tango so much, now is a lindy fiend.

The place where both sexes buy their spat-looking dance shoes is George's Shoes, 1604 W. Magnolia in Burbank. The phone number is (818) 955-7706.

They are still having salsa classes at the Sportsman's Lodge. Albert is still teaching a beginner class early and the band, arriving later, is (at least from what I saw the one time I went) in the fast and faster mode, one big blur that my friend Frank Cook's wife, Marcia, calls "salsa rock and roll."

All the people who used to go to El Floridita (the Mambo Society legion), this great Cuban nightclub on Monday nights where Johnny Polenca's band played, still go. Even though really it's so crowded that if you have feet, you have to watch out because girls wearing terrible high heels will crunch into you and you'll walk with a limp for six months or longer. (All dancers have podiatrists.)

Renée Victor, La Mujer Divina, teaches small but excellent beginner's salsa in a studio. It's on Burbank (near Vineland), with the beginner's class on Tuesday night at 8:00 P.M. At least when she's not away teaching Andy Garcia, Gena Rowlands, or whomever else the movie studios have in mind who has to look like they know what they're doing.

In Cahoots, sadly, has closed and is no longer in Glendale, but Paul McClure still teaches at the Western Connection in San Dimas, Friday nights and Sunday nights. Sunday nights are the "all two-step crowd," he says. He no longer produces the Riverside Country Dance event, being too busy. He has turned that over to someone else.

Sad, but even sadder, Dennis, the guy you used to be able to call to deliver your Evenin' Stars, those boots I was so crazy about, died. However, Paul McClure found out where they come from: Evenin' Star Pro Dance Boots, Gonzalas, Texas. The phone number is (830) 672-9591.

Most people in the country dance world don't die young, like people who went to Studio 54, so really, I was dismayed to hear he had died. But then, maybe, like me, he just was having brunch and then sort of exploded, I can't say for sure.

He didn't seem the kind who'd try lighting a cigar in his car and besides, he didn't have a VW bug; he drove one of those vans or SUVs like everyone else in two-step. He sold those boots out of the back of his van.

Saddest of all, for me, was the end of the Crest Lounge in Receda. It was named Crest, it seems, because when it started the idea of crests were what car clubs and guys like that thought was cool. A crest was used on their placards, and of course nobody who heard the word *crest* thought of toothpaste. Back then, Crest toothpaste hadn't even been invented.

So when I called information and heard there was no Crest anymore—it wasn't listed—I got in my car and drove all the way out there. Triumphantly, I managed to discover that it was still there and Sonny Watson was still teaching West Coast Swing on Tuesday nights, but now it's called the Jitterbug Lounge.

Not that anyone there would ever do jitterbug, because on Tuesday nights, I was told when I called this new number, Sonny Watson teaches West Coast Swing. Always has, always will. Or at least I hope so.

On Sunday nights, at Pasión (a block and a half west of Laurel Canyon at 12215 Ventura Boulevard), Sandra Giles still has her West Coast Swing nights. The class is taught by one of their regulars, and people still go there, because of course, Pasión is gorgeous and not such a schlep. Whereas the Crest, now the Jitterbug, is hideous and much too far into Receda for most people to go, never mind the parking and how easy the place is to miss if you've never been there. Pasión has a drawing of a tango couple on its marquee, and though it's upstairs in a minimall, the neighborhood, Studio City, is much less of a cold shower than Receda.

Not that, if you are a dancer, you expect to find anyplace half so nice as Pasión, which, on Tuesday nights, has tango and is so easy to take. Even its enemies admit that the floor, newly installed and made for actual dancers (unlike the Atlas, which was beautiful but had the tragic flaw), is all tango people or anyone, really, could ask for.

But I am sure that complaining about the Atlas being no longer a place where you can actually dance with a movie of great old dancers on the upper wall will not bring it back. And even if it did, everyone would complain because the floor is cement and ruins not only your feet but your shoes. A cement floor is something few dancers will overlook. Most are fiercely determined to spare their dance shoes, and they won't even wear them to get into a place if they have to walk on cement.

Anyway, the Atlas is still open; it's always there for people to go at night and have dinner—even though you have to use valet parking or everything in your car, or even your car itself, will be stolen, because the neighborhood is so problematic. In Studio City, you can park at Pasión, and your car will pretty surely be there when you come out. The Atlas was built in the same building that the Wiltern Theater is now in, the place for concerts by great acts and artists, which somehow revived an old movie theater into a great new place.

My sentiments exactly.

And Johnny Crawford is in a movie called *The Thirteenth*

Floor, out in May 1999, a science fiction adventure murder mystery. The hero goes back in time to 1937, and Johnny, playing at the Biltmore, does four numbers.

Today, Johnny and his band often work in the Cicada restaurant in the old Oviatt Building, a historic landmark, the first art deco office building in Los Angeles, built in 1928. It used to be the Ritz restaurant (when it opened it was a men's haberdashery store and thus had built-in drawers all over the walls, adding a wonderful sweetness to the place). It's a block from the Biltmore, and is now where Johnny (no longer doing the Hollywood Athletic Club as he was in Elmore Leonard's latest novel) usually does gigs.

The only thing that hasn't changed a lick is the Derby, except that Tiffany Brown is no longer teaching; she's off working for some designer, probably being an inspiration. The Derby is about the only place in L.A. besides the Atlas that has improved with the arrival of the present. This is because though it was first built in the twenties as one of the Brown Derbys and was somewhat popular, it ended up as Michael's, this restaurant in Los Feliz that wasn't that great. Nobody knew what lay under that dour exterior, a brown derby hat made of wood, and when the Derby people took over, maybe five or more years ago, it was once more revealed in all its glory. The past in the present, at least for now.

They took out the boring ceiling and left in the hat's insides, which are amazing, like some kind of great ski lodge, all wood, with a great bar and a too-small dance floor that you could get killed on if you don't watch out.

In the back of the Derby where the new people, not Tiffany, teach "swing" now, the whole place has had a new floor installed. It's so great that nobody wants to leave it and go out to the part where the bands play, even though they love the bands and wish they were playing on a floor you didn't get killed on.

The Derby is the one place that didn't change a hair once it opened. People still crowd to the beginners' dance class and love it because it's so easy you can learn all the moves in only an hour (something men are happy about, since what man wants to spend more than an hour learning anything, much less moves?).

The Cajun dance place hasn't changed either that much except that the gumbo people are never there anymore. When I asked for the nineteenth time where they were and was told "they're sick" I finally figured they're not sick; they're never coming back again as long as we live. Their food wasn't that great, not great like my gumbo or my mother's, but it was still something to eat you could put hot sauce on and it made the whole thing more rollicking and ridiculous. Now you have to wait for the music to start to feel anywhere near rollicking and silly.

Cajun dancers, of all the dancers, actually like food. They don't consider it an insult, the way other dancers do, and it was great sitting around at those big picnic tables, eating rice and beans, and drinking Pepsi with kids and old people and everyone else.

It struck me as a big loss when I figured out they weren't coming back ever. Still, it's a great place because even the one time I went back since my accident, the people were still nice. It was totally fun and everyone was there for one reason only, to dance the night away. I immediately tried to find John, the great waltz partner from Cal Tech, but he didn't arrive until I was leaving, and he was eating a pomegranate so he couldn't dance yet.

That place still has the second and fourth Friday of every month as Cajun dance night and once I get better, I'm going back. I tried doing one of their funny lessons, but got too sweaty in too short a time.

One of the good things about being a dancer is that you can dance in your head, even if you're in a hospital. The day it happened, I thought my legs just looked a little on the charred side; I didn't think it would mean I'd be almost dead.

Since I began dancing, what I really wanted to be was good enough that if Patrick Swayze asked me to do a waltz or a cha-cha, I would be able to. I knew I'd never be good enough to do a mambo with him, because nowadays with most mambos you can't hear the two unless you are a percussionist or otherwise adept at perceiving weird rhythmic signals. My friend Frank Cook who used to be the drummer in Canned Heat can hear anything if it is loud enough. When he came to take salsa lessons, hearing the two was nothing at all to him. It was just right there, in the congas or something.

Me, I can't hear the two and as for salsa itself, I'd rather dance it with Hugh, my cousin's former and current boyfriend. (They got back together after their episodic "troubles." Now Hugh's so great at dancing he can fake it for almost four or five hours before he, like me, no longer finds the energy to dance that well anymore.) Laurie and Hugh can go out to the hippest salsa places, and Laurie can dance with him. She no longer demands a man who can talk in a charming way and fix all her furniture as well as dance on the two till the cows come home. She's compromised her position.

"And besides," she told me, "you know, Art was a great musician, he could hear any beat. But what good did that do?"

"Right," I agreed. "After all, what good's a man who can hear anything if he's dead!"

The funny thing is that there have always been people in Los

Angeles who insist on going out, being "in the scene" (whichever one you choose), finding colorful groups of people, music, charm, and adventure. Most of those today who aren't dead (scenes get dead because the people in them, they don't notice their health, you might say) have somehow stopped their downward plummet. They either get sober or they follow the medical advice that if they don't do something, they're going to be dead or, worse yet, fatter.

In Los Angeles, you can't be fat and feel good about things, it's just impossible. So if you find yourself sober and worried about your looks, going dancing is the best thing to do. Most people I know are just too neurotic to find actual exercise anything but too boring.

The singles scene has so worn out its welcome that no one who isn't two sails to the wind can stand these bars anymore. Once they realize just how abysmal it all is, they are often drawn to these wonderful dance scenes, the lessons, meeting new people just as rotten as they are, the ambition to be as one with the music, the night, and someone, maybe you.

For me, doing this book got me into such great shape, I managed to survive being half done in, half gone. Even though today I have a real medical explanation as to why I can't stand high heels and if I do dance, it's going to be only in moccasins, it still seems to me that one day I'll get back in my great boots and look at least credible. But as for now, it's moccasins or die.

Luckily, my feet came out okay. My ankles weren't wrecked, just the rest of me up to my waist, which makes it feel as though I'm wearing too-tight Capri pants, too uncomfortable to rise above it and just be one with the music.

However, Maurice and I have gone dancing a couple of times, and doing fox-trot, I can just forget about it all.

And luckily now that I don't have to wear high heels, the tango is so much easier. I can't begin to thank God for this excuse never to wear high heels again.

The blond hair I had to represent the past, i.e., Hollywood blondes, is now gone. I'm back to my original hair color, a normal brown, sort of ash color, which lately has seemed to be in style. Since I do have brown eyes as well as eyebrows, having brown hair too, well, it looks natural, you might even say.

Since I myself am lucky enough, when I go dancing, not to be looking for anything but a dance, it doesn't matter if my hair is no longer so neon it is bound to attract just anyone, even people I don't know. Besides, now that I have actually written this book and it is going to appear, it's all the publicity I need.

The thing about partner or social dancing is that even though on the one hand it can be completely about who are the best dancers in the room, it can also, if you find the right crowd like I did when I went to Cajun dancing, be fun. People can be nice to you, won't find you wanting (well, Cajuns would have a lot of nerve, finding anyone worse than they are), and even if you don't find anyone to be madly in love with, it's a lot better than most places people go to, looking for companionship. Because most of the time, you have too much fun to notice you're getting exercise.

I am lucky to move in various other social lives, and have lots of friends who are perfectly good even if they don't dance. But then there's the other side; the dances with someone like Maurice who can make you feel so smooth. It's almost like flying, only better, because when it's over, you don't have to deplane.

Maurice has showed me a lot of clippings he saved from the olden days when to have a social life, you had to dance. Arthur

Murray, the dance studio, ran the social life of most people in America, teaching them to dance and running ads everywhere saying things like "If you can walk, you can dance" or "I went from being a wallflower to having a whole new bunch of friends, after only six weeks of dance lessons."

For a long time I wanted to call this book *I Went from Being a Wallflower to Dancing Every Night of the Week, After Only Nine Years of Dance Lessons.*

But they wouldn't let me; it's too wordy for a book title. And they wouldn't let me call it *You and the Night and the Music* because it's too personal; people would be mad when it didn't turn out to be about them and the night and the music.

My friend Tandy Martin said, "Call it *Two by Two*, it's at least graphic, they could see it in a bookstore."

"But what if they think it's about boards?" I protested. "You know, two-by-fours, right? Carpentry?"

"There will be dancing on the cover," she explained, "*Two by Two*, don't ask me to explain, I just know it's what will work."

"What if they think it's Noah's Ark?" another protester said. "You know, the animals going onto the ark? Weren't they two by two too?"

"Maybe we can have zebras doing the tango!" I said, "All those hooves?"

It's funny because when I wrote *Sex and Rage*, my first novel, the thing that kept me from deciding I could never finish, that I wasn't a novelist and what was I doing writing a book so long when all I really could write were short stories, was a strange car ornament or something my friend Paul Ruscha found for me. Cast in bronze with a kind of gold overlay, it was a couple, oddly enough dancing the tango.

Looking forward to seeing that couple dancing on the cover of my book, which my editor had promised I could have if I ever, indeed, finished, forced me to get it over with. Just so that tango couple could be used in a photograph Paul Ruscha took. The fact that he shot the statue in the bathtub and it had raindrops on it from the shower was an added plus in my opinion.

The odd thing about that tango couple was that the woman's head was always falling off. I glue it back on with Crazy Glue, but no matter how often I do it still falls off, causing me to think that in the world of men and women dancing, the woman's head is always going to roll, or at least be temporarily in need of Crazy Glue—where the tango is concerned anyway.

Today, the world of tango is still filled with too many women, and the world of ballroom dancing, where you can at least just do a fox-trot and not worry too much about balance, is not filled enough with anyone (outside of a few diehards like Mark and Maurice) who can do a fox-trot to simple romantic music and make it smooth enough to float you off the floor.

Most women, of course, would be satisfied if we were back in the old days when you could find some man who knew, at least, how to slow-dance and could do it to great old mushy songs— the ones I grew up listening to, like "Earth Angel" or "Over the Mountain."

When I was in junior high, those were the songs I longed to dance at the school "social dances" they had where even during lunchtime, teachers would be on the alert, making sure we weren't getting too close, even though that's really all we were there for.

The other popular dance at my school in L.A. back then was a pachuco kind of swing dance called the Choke. The girl rolled in and out quickly on her heels, and the guy just stood there, seemingly with one hand tied behind his back, hardly moving at all, just staring out the windows into the smog. Back then, there were teachers trying to get that dance erased from our minds because in their opinion, pachuco style was the wrong thing to aim for. They wanted us to be pert types who did regular East Coast–type swing, sort of an Americanized cleaned-up version, where girls and boys seemed to move in sync, smiling. Pachucos never smiled, they were too immersed in their dance; smiling didn't occur to them.

Later, when I was nineteen and living in Rome for six months, I ran into this kid I'd known from those days. Except now he was not longer a pachuco, but rather the Dominican Republic consul to Rome, his family having overthrown whoever had been there before and now themselves running things. He was telling me this at this great party in an embassy where everyone was in tuxedos or, like me, wearing a brocaded satin, A-line dress, when suddenly "Runaround Sue" came on, which had just become a hit.

"You want to, uh, dance?" he asked me.

Suddenly he assumed that pachuco posture, I became "the girl," and we were off, doing the Choke, me rolling into and out of his arms, his tuxedo suddenly no longer the most classic thing about him. There we were, two kids whose aspiration to dance like pachucos was finally paying off. The crowd parted, everyone was stunned, we got applause at the end, people were so amazed.

If all we'd done was swing like everyone else, we would never have wowed them in Rome. But Rome is a place that knows something great when they see it and the Choke, the only partner dance I ever wanted to do if I couldn't be slow-dancing, was great.

Today, of course, I know only one person, Sydney (one of the better tango dancers, and great at Latin too), who, because she too went to Le Conte Junior High when I did, remembers how fun that dance was and wishes it was still here.

My friend Jim Hines said, "There are some songs you can dance to, and some songs you *must* dance to." For me, whenever I hear that Etta James song "At Last" that they play now for the Jaguar commercials, I feel I must dance. It's the ultimate slow one, the ultimate "last dance," the ultimate trouble you can "at last" get into. But the great thing about dancing, at least for women, is that unlike sex, you don't get anything except danced with.

My favorite dance movie isn't any of the tango ones they have now or anything like *Dance with Me* where all the extras are Albert Torres and his specialists. My favorite is *Dirty Dancing*, the one with Patrick Swayze teaching Jennifer Grey to do the mambo in order to do a show so his usual partner won't be missed, and she can sneak off and get an abortion the only day the traveling abortionist is going to be there. To me, that movie was perfect. It had the great old Jewish Catskill life down pat, it had the women using waiters and dance instructors for romance, it had the parents not knowing anything that was going on though it was right under their noses, and it had those great slow-dancing numbers, the dirty dancing, which we, at our school, were trying to sneak into our school dances but couldn't because we were always found out by vigilant chaperones.

Plus it had Patrick Swayze, who, the first time I saw him, was in one of those skateboard movies where he played a villain who danced on roller skates, doing all these gorgeous ballet routines, only on skates. And he was so gorgeous. The guy who took me to see the movie, a casting director named Fred Roos, cast him in that movie *The Outsiders* Coppola directed, the one where all the guys were so cute it was hard to see how much cuter Swayze was.

Of course, for me, if he's not dancing or doing tai chi, forget it, he's doing the wrong thing. And the truth is, he's really a dancer;

he danced in that New York ballet company. So if he wants to lower himself to mambo, who are we to complain, especially when he's in color and all tan with those green-blue eyes.

I think the reason Patrick Swayze so devastated people who saw *Dirty Dancing* was that, like Valentino, he was able to look at a woman and not flinch or cave or whatever most men do looking at women. If you dance in ballet, you have to look at your partner, so it's probably just trained deep into him, to pull this off so unflinchingly.

Most men, even in movies, seem to act like holding a woman's gaze is just too beneath them for words, too much like being on their side, like having given up. Dancers, men who lead women in partner dancing, have to learn both to look at the woman and to dance. This can take quite some time.

For me, what happened in the hospital was bad, but having something to look forward to made it possible to survive. Having been through humiliation and varieties of spiritual despair, being unable for so long even to follow, I was in the perfect frame of mind to do whatever a physical therapist told me, no matter how horrible it was. Moving across a bed, getting on a walker (!), that whole grisly and ugly bunch of stuff—all nothing, having done salsa.

The funniest thing was, for almost a year before the accident, my knee gave out trying to do West Coast Swing and I thought it would never ever stop hurting. I found out that instead of going and having knee operations like my cousin does, if you lie down in the ICU for six weeks and are totally bedridden another two months, why, your knee hardly hurts at all. In fact, since this happened my knee is all better.

INDEX